To: our beloved
Acharya Susane
Chapman
Susmita Banner.
Lexington 2.17.19

THE *Power* OF *Life Coaching*
VOLUME 2

MANIFESTING TRANSFORMATION IN FINANCIAL, PROFESSIONAL, EMOTIONAL, SPIRITUAL, WELLNESS AND RELATIONSHIP ASPECTS

Barbara Wainwright

BALBOA PRESS
A DIVISION OF HAY HOUSE

Copyright © 2018 Barbara Wainwright.

All rights reserved. No part of this book may be used or reproduced by any means, graphic, electronic, or mechanical, including photocopying, recording, taping or by any information storage retrieval system without the written permission of the author except in the case of brief quotations embodied in critical articles and reviews.

Balboa Press books may be ordered through booksellers or by contacting:

Balboa Press
A Division of Hay House
1663 Liberty Drive
Bloomington, IN 47403
www.balboapress.com
1 (877) 407-4847

Because of the dynamic nature of the Internet, any web addresses or links contained in this book may have changed since publication and may no longer be valid. The views expressed in this work are solely those of the author and do not necessarily reflect the views of the publisher, and the publisher hereby disclaims any responsibility for them.

The author of this book does not dispense medical advice or prescribe the use of any technique as a form of treatment for physical, emotional, or medical problems without the advice of a physician, either directly or indirectly. The intent of the author is only to offer information of a general nature to help you in your quest for emotional and spiritual well-being. In the event you use any of the information in this book for yourself, which is your constitutional right, the author and the publisher assume no responsibility for your actions.

Any people depicted in stock imagery provided by Getty Images are models, and such images are being used for illustrative purposes only.
Certain stock imagery © Getty Images.

Print information available on the last page.

ISBN: 978-1-9822-0457-0 (sc)
ISBN: 978-1-9822-0456-3 (hc)
ISBN: 978-1-9822-0458-7 (e)

Library of Congress Control Number: 2018906029

Balboa Press rev. date: 06/11/2018

Contents

Preface vii

The Power is Already Within You 1

Health, Wellness and Healing 8

Dealing With Death 14

A Power Greater Than Ourselves Can Restore Our Faith 21

Architects for Health 28

Regain Health through Mind, Body, Spirit Coaching 36

What Are You Working So Hard For? 43

The Importance of an Academic Life Coach 50

Stay Present. Live in the Now 58

Igniting the Inner Coach, Light Body to Awaken Self 64

Life Coaching and The Power of Leading Questions 70

Financial Coaching: Blending Financial
Planning Analytics with the Art of Life Coaching 76

Relationship Coaching 82

Addiction Is Just a Symptom of a Bigger Problem 89

Spiritual Coaching: A Metaphysical Approach to Self Love .. 96

AfterWord 103

Preface

In our second edition of the Power of Life Coaching Book, fifteen Certified Professional Coaches from Wainwright Global, Institute of Professional Coaching came together to share their coaching experiences with the world. We all have a passion for life coaching and appreciate the transformational experiences we have the privilege to share with each our clients. Each of us are motivated to provide excellent coaching services that result in men and women living an inspired life they love, a fulfilling life, because we help individuals to live from their heart, with passion.

The authors of this book, bare their souls, as they share their personal stories of struggle and their triumphs over them. Each life coach empowers their clients in their own special way. My hope is that you will feel a connection with these life coaches, and that you will be motivated to reach out to them.

These life coaches provide life coaching services many different genres:

• Academic Coaching	• Mind, Body, Spirit Coaching
• C-Level Executive Coaching	• Mindfulness Coaching
• Christian Life Coaching	• Personal Development Coaching
• Clinical Health Coaching	
• Grief Coaching	• Recovery Coaching
• Financial Coaching	• Relationship Coaching
• Health, Wellness and Healing Coaching	• Retirement Coaching
	• Spiritual Coaching

My intention for creating this book collaboration is to help you understand what life coaching is and the many different areas that life coaches can be of assistance in. There are over 52 coaching niches that Wainwright Global Certified Professional Life Coaches specialize in. So whether you would appreciate improvements in your life, financially, professionally, spiritually, physically, emotionally, or in your relationships, a life coach can help you gain clarity of your best path and will encourage and motivate you to arrive at your chosen destination.

I'd like to thank all the coaches that contributed to this book: Woody Goulart, Shari Salomon, Larry Thomas, Jr., Tonya Hunter-Hurst, William K. Appelgate, Debra Simon, Doug Jarvie, Dawn A. Peters-Bascombe, Paul Sahota, Susmita Barua, David Cary, Holley G. Cary, Gregory Charles, and Jon Wainwright. I'd also like to thank Heath Chadwick for his much appreciated assistance with the creation of this book. It takes a lot of tenacity and dedication to create a book, or even a chapter in a book. I am grateful to all these professionals who made this book possible.

The Power is Already Within You
By Woody Goulart

"The inner you powers the outer you. This is an essential trait you may never have realized you already have inside of you." ~ Woody Goulart

---

We all go spinning around the sun together using the same 525,600 minutes required to make that essential journey. Why do some people appear to be experiencing a greater level of happiness and fulfillment than others as time goes by?

I know their secrets. What separates the happy and fulfilled ones from all the rest starts with a simple spark.

Examining the Spark

My father's father taught me what to look for. The spark was very clear for me to see within my grandfather. In contrast, I saw several people throughout my life who "lost their spark," so to speak, as the years passed. I wanted different dreams for myself that would enable me to feel truly alive.

How did my paternal grandfather retain his spark? I believe I now know the answer.

He was an immigrant from the Azores Islands in the North Atlantic. When he was a child, he entered the United States by way of Ellis Island with my great-grandfather. My grandfather was an adventurous man. I grew to admire him for that. His life spanned nearly 80 years, most of which were spent in Central California.

He earned his personal wealth from real estate holdings, but he saw himself as a rancher and a fisherman. Crops of vegetables were grown on his land and then harvested by farm workers. He also raised livestock over most of his life.

My grandfather went fishing on the Pacific Ocean for recreation and relaxation but fishing also was a way to put food on our table. During my preteen years my entire family accompanied my grandfather up to Humboldt County in Northern California for salmon fishing.

My grandfather, my father, and his brother would all go salmon fishing and then bring back the catch of the day to the campground near the ocean where we had our vacation trailers parked. Apparently, I was not destined to be a fisherman. I was too young to go out on the ocean with the grown men and participate in what I guessed were some secret rituals to capture fish.

I always had a vivid imagination. Instead of bravely facing the adventures I imagined were out there on the sea, I stayed on the shore. There I played cowboys and soldiers with other boys my age as we used pretend guns that we fashioned out of tree branches to enable our pretend violence.

Living the Dream

I developed a deep respect for my rancher/fisherman grandfather. Much of the admiration I felt for him came from witnessing how hard he worked. As he grew older, my grandfather diminished his direct involvement in ranching and instead chose to focus on spending time out on the ocean.

My grandfather was a man who did what he wanted after he saw it in his mind. He never showed any signs that he dreamed about the traditional United States concept of quietly growing older and retiring. He died peacefully out on the Pacific Ocean while fishing in a small boat.

I grew up within a very different social environment compared to my grandfather. My generation came to appreciate longer life expectancies compared to previous centuries. But, few people I knew had any plans for what to do with those "extra years."

I learned many life lessons growing up that guide me today in my professional coaching. Today I offer people ways to make time work for us each day instead of worrying that time is running away too fast.

New Dreams for a New Era

We live in the present era with amazing technology and advances in personal comforts that would have seemed to us when we were kids like they come from science fiction. Yet, much of what my generation learned from school and society has conditioned us to abide by yesterday's predictable patterns in life. Such patterns include the opinion that once you reach a "certain age," you should stop working for a living and just relax in leisure activities.

You put in your time at work. Maybe you changed jobs once or twice. Mainly, you put in your time. I know that's what I did. After all those years, did I feel happier? No, I did not.

Today I coach people not to expect to retire from the world of work someday but instead to aim for a restart. In very simple terms, here it is: Restart versus retire.

I have restarted my life and career several times. I would never recommend something unless I had tried it personally. Initially I was a radio broadcaster working in Hollywood. Then, I got my master's degree and doctoral degree and worked as a university professor. I transitioned into a career in new technology in what we now call the broadband industry. Then, I was fortunate to work in Washington, DC in a leadership role in coaching executive communication.

All my multiple restarts were made possible because of what I held in my mind as possible for me. Most of us came up through the world of work similarly. We consistently paid part of our wages into the federal Social Security program. Why? Well, tax laws give us little choice. But, mostly, we all bought into the American dream. That's what I did.

For years it seemed to be a comforting dream to embrace. Like many other, I saw myself in the future with gray hair and wisdom. I would play golf or tennis on the days when I was not busy getting hair transplants or color treatments.

There we are in the possible future drinking ice tea (or perhaps a much stronger variation that includes vodka and tequila) while resting barefooted on the front porch of a beachfront cottage with our significant other. The two of us smile at the young schoolchildren who walk by in utter dread from their painful lives shaped by oblivious parents.

Our smiles in this dream mainly come from one simple, but comforting fantasy: One day in the future we would no longer need to go to work. No more facing that grumpy boss. No more annoying coworkers. No more commute. No more business attire. No more computers. Best of all, no more dealing with younger people who type on small hand-held devices using only their thumbs.

We've dreamed of transitioning from the world of work into the world of relaxation and leisure. Ah, what a lovely dream! Oh, what bliss this dream can bring. In the dream, we effortlessly sail into creature comforts in our "golden years" accompanied by the soothing soundtrack of silly McCartney love songs.

Envision Your Life and Embrace What You Envision

The legendary American comic Joan Rivers celebrated 81 birthdays. In her later years she very clearly stated her strong preference to keep on working until the day she died. The night before her life ended so tragically during a failed medical procedure, Joan Rivers performed in front of a live audience. Such behavior often gets called self-fulfilling prophecy. But, it is not really a prophecy at all. It is your mental equivalent of your life that tends to propel you towards the destiny that your mind envisions.

How you picture the way your life is going, and, how you picture the way your life will go are both crucially important. The life that you picture in your mind makes all the difference in your happiness each day that you are alive.

That's what my coaching does. I show you how the pictures you keep in your mind can keep you feeling good about your life experiences. It all starts when you discover the proven ways to keep how you picture your life working for you rather than against you.

The simple trick in this is to take control over what you picture in your mind each day to attract happiness in your life and ward off unhappiness.

Secrets of Life

So, you want to learn life's secrets? Okay, fair enough. I can tell you that you may find it when you start with a fresh focus upon the space between your ears.

How you come across in life is directly connected to how you "see yourself" in your mind (not when you look in a mirror.) You should take specific actions to align what's in your mind (your self-image) with how you would like to appear to others in the physical world. There is no reason for anyone to allow a self-image inside their mind to be left to chance or accident. But, learning how to take control of your mind's image of yourself is not really a secret at all.

Almost anyone can learn the core truth about this life: The inner you powers the outer you.

This is not hocus-pocus within what previously was called "mind over matter." At the heart of all my coaching is a simple concept that some people never master. I guide you to arrive at a point when you work with your mind and use it rather than allowing your mind to work against you and use you up.

I will never promise that you can "live happily ever after" as the fables of our youth made us all hope for. But, I will show you how your happiness in life is within reach starting with what you picture in your mind each day. This is an essential trait you may never have realized you already have inside of you.

Meet Coach Woody Goulart

Today I am a certified professional coach. I restarted my career in coaching and consulting to serve people on a personal, individual basis following decades of coaching, consulting, training and mentoring within major organizations with large corporate structures.

I earned my doctoral degree from Indiana University, Bloomington, plus I also have a master's degree and a bachelor's degree from the California State University system. For nearly two decades I held leadership roles in coaching executive communications at the national office of AARP and at federal agencies in the District of Columbia including Headquarters, Department of the Army, and the Departments of Defense and Justice.

I have a managerial track record in the commercial broadcasting and broadband industries in major media markets including Los Angeles and Boston. I have taught at the university level online and in classrooms including in the National Capital Region. My husband and I have been together for more than 20 years. We are residents of Las Vegas, Nevada, where we were married.

To learn more about me go to http://CoachWoody.Vegas where you can download my free eBook, enroll in my free online course, plus much more.

Health, Wellness and Healing

USING ESSENTIAL OILS, SUPERFOODS, SUPPLEMENTS, AND WORKOUTS

By Shari Salomon

"I really do see the good, underneath the layers of fear in most people. I find people put on a protective coating. I help them ease through the process of peeling away those rough layers to find their optimal health, healing, and wellness." ~ Shari Salomon

---

As this new chapter is being written, it is running parallel to a new chapter in my career. I am a Master Life Coach, and my specialty is in Health, Healing, and Wellness. I have been asked to share my knowledge with others and I am beyond flattered actually. I am now ready to do that, as I have created the curriculum for a coaching course focused on Health, Healing and Wellness. I am teaching and training individuals interested in health, healing and wellness in how to use the same skills I have learned to help my clients heal their aches and pains, lose weight and feel good about their lives. And now, with much success under my belt, I have put all my expertise into a program that I am grateful to be able to offer to others. I am willing and able to share my abilities with others; to help others to find ways to answer questions they did not even know existed.

I thrive while working with people. Although I was not always confident in myself, I have learned to believe and trust in myself, through the many facets of coaching, learning new coping skills, life skills and asking myself those most unwanted questions. I have found the people in my life that I surround myself with, are my most important and endearing quality. These are the people I call LIFELINES. These people are in my life because we serve a mutual purpose of some kind to each other. The people you reach out to when the "chips are down", when all you want to do is scream for help, these are those people. They are present in my life for a mutual purpose, but not necessarily needed on a regular basis. These people would drop everything to be with me, and I the same for them.

I believe knowing this about myself is important, striving to be open and completely honest, telling you the truth, as it is presented in front of me. Even if it is not what you wanted to know or hear. Some people would not call that their best quality or mine. Personally, I think it may be, only even mine alone. Never looking to hurt or offend anyone. Although most likely, it is why we encountered each other, why you have likely put someone, like me in your life. This quality in me may be the reason we came together. Admittedly, life moves very quickly and time flies even quicker. We don't always get a chance to savor the important moments. We don't necessarily have to relate to time by a calendar or the clock. So having a life coach to guide you on your way is a very positive step to overall wellness.

The new curriculum embraces you as a Life Coach or to becoming a Life Coach, with a specialty in Health, Healing, and Wellness. You will learn about your optimal health, through various food options. What makes your body unique is you. As a Health Coach, I help you to find what foods work for your individual body as well as what foods clutter the thoughts in your head. We work together to get you out of the brain fog you may be feeling.

Healing works your ability to learn the fundamentals of meditation, introducing you to different types of meditation as well as their benefits. Meditation can take you on amazing journeys. Learning meditation, to move and share healing energy, can free your body and mind. Sharing with others will bring great joy.

Wellness has us working with Essential Oils, Superfoods, Supplements, and Workouts. These all fascinate me. I love challenging my brain to keep learning, experimenting and rewarding my brain with knowledge. I love to share my essential oils with my clients, family, and friends. I have a daily mix of many oils I use every day, and other oils many times a day. This is all for my optimal wellness. I am always carrying my essential oils with me, just in case anyone may need something for a headache, congestion or even a bee sting. I am passionate about oiling and love to share information about its healing properties.

Get ready to learn how superfoods can be the pick me up to get you through your day. We learn about the top, most beneficial, natural, foods that can help to heal our bodies. We explore many different real food options that you can also get in supplement form too.

Easy to share workouts that you can easily demonstrate to your clients. These will help to keep them motivated and active while you are working together. The workouts require nothing but the desire to do them and your own body to perform them. I only ask my clients to work to the best of their ability always.

The Questions:

Who, What, When, Where, How, and Why, did this all start?

Starting in order, it always starts with me, my surroundings and the need to want to keep my mind focused on new challenges and my mind busy. I love to take new certifications and thought a concentration in recovery or relationships was my next focus. So the **WHO** goes like this; I turned to Barbara Wainwright, who immediately reached back to me knowing I was ready for a new challenge. She asked about my coaching practice and was ready to help in any way possible. The conversation went like this: Can you help me decide which program is more what I am looking for? Barbara took the time to talk me through both courses that interested me, and after much debate on my side, I had the passion and readiness to take on Recovery Coaching. I was looking to somehow better help others who have family members that are addicts. This is where Jon Wainwright came into my story. Jon is my Master Recovery Coach. Jon fascinated me with his knowledge. Jon has amazing passion as well as patience, to teach this program. I found myself able to confide my stories with him as he shared the same with his own stories. In a conversation with Jon, he mentioned that Barbara did channeling and maybe she could help to answer some of my questions regarding my suffering with depression.

Here is the **What**, that brought me where we are today. Well, right Jon was. I scheduled an appointment to find out about channeling, so many questions were answered immediately that day. The handwritten notes I have from that session with Barbara and her medium in which she channels through look like chicken scratch, all over the paper. I found out I am a healer of "some sort" and my fight with depression is from not being able to live out past lives to the fullest. Once that sunk in, I was ready to explore even more. I had such a passion for the knowledge that was being shared with me. When those feelings of depression come now I am able to be more understanding of myself, more aware to share and communicate with those lifelines I referred to earlier in this chapter.

So the **When**, was the spring of 2017, everything unraveled in this channeling session and I was destined to hear more. Scheduled another session with Barbara, where we also, talked about my readiness to become a Master Coach, the Channel said NO, that is not your purpose. I was crushed, admittedly completely crushed.

Where was I heading with this career path if not a Master Coach? I love to teach so wouldn't this be the next step? The path the Channel put me on was never even on the radar. Now I was being told the only way to heal myself, was to start to heal others and to teach others how to heal as well. So that is where the Health, Healing and Wellness curriculum came about. The Channel told me to do it, and Barbara was as surprised as I was. She had always wanted to offer a course like this but never had anyone to take on the challenge.

How do I start? I know basic meditation practices. I started with a few friends needing to learn meditation. Adding it to my already existing practice of Life/Nutrition/Recovery and now Meditation Coaching, I sat down for a course in Reiki I, II, and Master level. I loved learning another way to heal others and now use my Reiki knowledge often for myself and my clients, friends, and even my husband.

So the next infamous question is **Why**? My roles are plenty. I am a mother of three amazing young women, just embarking on adulthood.

Each of them is on their own career path. I also have a completely supportive husband as my best friend and my successful studio practice. I see my clients for Life, Nutritional, Recovery Coaching, Personal Training, Meditation, Yoga, Spinning, Core Balance. What more could I want or need? This is the answer for me. I have a need to share. We embark on people, places at certain times in our lives. There are many people I see now as clients for various reasons. Some that I have known all my life, others from grade school, high school, people I have just met for a reason and we are drawn to each other. The answer to my hardest most challenging question is the WHY? This is the question I am constantly asking myself. I can only answer it as follows: I believe in many people, more than I find they believe in themselves. I really do see the good, underneath the layers of fear in most people. I find people put on a protective coating. I work hard to help them ease through the process of peeling away those rough layers to find their optimal Health, Healing, and Wellness.

Coach Shari Salomon

Shari Salomon is the owner of 121 for Life. She is a Master Coach of Health, Healing, and Wellness as well as a Certified Recovery Coach. As an avid gym lover since her teens, she has become a certified Personal Trainer, Spinning, Aqua, Core/Balance, Yoga instructor, Reiki Master and Meditational Coach. Shari was one of the very early users of "Virtual" training, using a webcam to train clients. She aspires to help all who come into her path for whatever their purpose. Shari is a firm believer that we all meet for a reason, and is constantly looking to find the answers as to "why?" Shari has been married to Michael for 24 years and she looks forward to spending many more years together with him as he has been the love of her life since becoming childhood sweethearts at the ages of 14 and 16. Together they have three beautiful and unique adult daughters, Sydney, Molli, and Mackenzie. With their love and support, "121 for Life" was created and has begun to successfully thrive. Shari is forever grateful for her wonderful family and an amazing support system. To learn more, visit Shari's website at www.121forlife.com

Dealing With Death

How I Learned to Live Through It
By Coach Larry Thomas, Jr.

"Occasionally you'll lose, occasionally you'll win, but you're gonna fight." ~ Larry Thomas, Jr.

"Eventually, I realized I wasn't alone. My loved ones, although no longer here, were still with me in my mind and heart. It wasn't the same, but it's what I had left, and it was up to me to allow that to be enough."

So, here I am, 45 years old and on the other side of significant loss mostly due to the death of loved ones. Three deaths in particular: one that would change me, a second that almost broke me, and a third I was better prepared to find my way through.

I was five years old when my mother passed away. From what they told me, while she was hemorrhaging to death due to an allergic reaction to penicillin, she was instructing the family how they should take care of my older sister and me. I don't know how accurate that story is, but I like to believe, even in her dying moments, she loved me enough to think of me and my well-being. It's the best I can do when I imagine what my mother's love feels like. And that's important because at five years old I'm standing in front of my mother's casket, quietly staring at her motionless body, waiting, but deep down knowing, she's not getting up. There are people all around me, but I'm the loneliest little boy in the world. I'm standing there, and even then without knowing it, I was making a decision.

It's been over forty years since my mother passed. My memories of her are becoming blurry. Most of them are now bits and pieces; flashes of moments here and there. Some of them I'm trying to turn them into life lessons. That way the short time we had together feels like she was teaching me a thing or two.

I remember the time my sister got into a fight with the girl from down the street. During the struggle, she grabbed my sister by the hair and dug her on the sidewalk. The girl left, and my mother made us sit by the apartment door and wait for her to come back. I don't know who was crazier, my mother for having my sister sit there with bloody knees or the girl for actually coming back. This time, my sister fought with an entirely different purpose and when it looked like she was winning, my mother separated them, told the girl to go home, and told my sister to go in the house. My mother then calmed her down, cleaned her up, and sent her to bed. Now, it's not like she turned to me and explained what just happened, but I'd like to think she was telling me something: in life, you're going to lose some and win some, but you're always going to have to fight. I chuckle about it now, but I've been living that lesson. I've had my share of wins and loses and my victory has always been my willingness to keep fighting.

Time passes. Life happens.

I dropped out of college and moved back home because I was becoming a father. The baby was born, a few months passed, and we all moved in together. Now, saying I wasn't ready for all of that would be an understatement because not too long after, I broke up with my girlfriend and moved out. Sounds crazy, but after some months of adjusting, things were turning around and coming together for me. I started working a well-paying job, and I was beginning to resurface. I was coming up for air and appreciating the chance to breathe again. Sure, I was gasping and still a bit disoriented, but I was above water.

I was working at a small factory that supplied parts for the major auto manufacturers. Seven days a week, I'd go to work, stack my parts, move my parts, check my parts, move my parts again, take a break, and repeat the process. This job, as mundane as it was, was giving me hope that despite my numerous setbacks, I still had a chance. I should have been happy, but I was working seven days a week and working the second shift. I hadn't seen my daughter in a long time, and it was bothering me. So, I wasn't.

It was a Friday, and I called my now ex-girlfriend to let her know I was coming to pick my daughter up for the weekend. We were going to take daddy/daughter pictures. She told me our daughter recently had photos taken. She was planning to surprise me with them but, since she was getting her hair done, maybe we could all take pictures together on Sunday. That way, we'd have some family photos. It wasn't a bad idea, so I thought no problem.

The next day, I'm at work ranting and raving about not coming in tomorrow when the machines went down and production stopped. Whatever happened, they weren't able to get them back up running, so they let us go home. I got home and tried to catch up with my baby's mother. She was already in the middle of her day so, to pass the time, I started going through my phone book and logging my contacts into my computer. I'm calling quite a few numbers, and of course, they're asking about my daughter. You have to understand; I was the first from my circle of friends to become a father, so I'm on a path far removed from the plan. They just wanted to know I was okay. Then it happened. I got a call. There was an accident. They were going to the hospital. I left the house with a feeling in my stomach I hadn't felt in a long time and no idea where the hospital was.

After Daisha's funeral, I tried to go back to work, but I couldn't get it together. I lost my job, and I fell into a state of depression. The weight of it all was just too much for me. I keep thinking of my mother, all the other family members I had lost, and how unfair life was. On more than one occasion, I thought about checking out. Fortunately for me, I had a strong support circle made up of family and friends. My daughter's mother and I leaned on them and each other often. But, more than anything, I discovered I had experience. Not the "losing a child" part, but with "losing". I had this fight before and came back for more. If I did it then, I could do it again. Right?

After some time, I went back to working. It was a sales position, and to get to know my customers, I allowed them an opportunity to get to know me. I started opening up and sharing my story with complete strangers. Surprisingly enough, not only were they willing to listen, they were willing to share their own stories. I was amazed to hear so many filled with devastating circumstances and tragedies yet punctuated with victories, or at the very least commitments to keep fighting. Eventually, I realized I wasn't alone. My loved ones, although no longer here, were still with me in my mind and heart. It wasn't the same, but it's what I had left, and it was up to me to allow that to be enough. Did it hurt? Of course. It still does. But the question is: do you stop or keep living despite the hurt? That's the decision I was making.

Time passes. Life happens.

And then my dad died.

I became a graphic designer, and I often provide services to families or individuals in need of funeral programs. It was there, sitting with families who had just lost their loved ones, experiencing a significant shift in their reality, I found myself again sharing my story and the lessons I'd learned along the way. The following are ten beliefs, rules, or guidelines I've adopted and use to help me deal with my losses, as well as, assist me in my efforts to understand and relate to others:

1. There are powers and forces bigger and stronger than me.
2. Some things I won't understand, but I will have to accept.
3. When my reality changes, I'll have to change as well.
4. Everyone dies. It's the when, the where, the how, and the question of why that makes it difficult.
5. How they lived is more important than how they died.
6. I'm not the only one hurting, and mine is uniquely my own.
7. My level of hurt is often equal to my level of love.
8. I will have to define and articulate my hurt to heal.
9. I'm stronger than I believe.
10. Their legacy is my responsibility.

I became a "Life Coach" because I want to help. I know what it feels like to lose a loved one. I've felt the guilt, the resentment, the shame, the hopelessness, and all the stuff that comes with it. I even know what it feels like to lose yourself because of it. I want to help the person struggling to find their path, discover it for the first time. I want to help the person standing at the fork in their road, decide which way their journey continues. I want to help the person who may have gotten lost find their way again. As hard as my experiences were, I know what it feels like to figure out how to live despite that hurt and pain. And while I'm not saying MY answers are THE answers, I am saying the coaching process can help you find yours. The question is: "Are you looking and willing to work with someone to find them?" If so, let's talk about it.

Coach Larry Thomas, Jr.

Larry Thomas, Jr. is a personal development coach for men and women feeling frustrated from not living the life they are fully capable of living. He works to challenge you and your current way of thinking to expand your perspective and create doable action steps with a goal of increasing your success rates and getting you from where you are to where you want to be.

With a focus on one's life, leadership, and legacy, Larry works with clients committed to making the needed decisions and actions that potentially brings them closer to the goals of their choosing which equates to life more fulfilling and based on their actual intentions and purpose.

Known for his open, transparent, thought-provoking, unorthodox, and sometimes humorous approach, Larry will help you design the strategies needed to empower you and increase your chances of success. His teachings and stories are filled with life's ups, downs, triumphs, tragedies, and the moments in between that make all the difference.

Larry offers a wide range of coaching programs and services such as individual and group coaching, workshops, and speaking opportunities. Larry Thomas, Jr. can be contacted by visiting his website at www.larrythomasjunior.com.

Larry is also the founder and owner of The Inner Link (a graphic design and print company), speaker, aspiring author, mentor, father, and friend.

A Power Greater Than Ourselves Can Restore Our Faith

By Tonya Hunter-Hurst

In life, you should look in the mirror and not at others. In the blame game nobody wins. ~ Tonya Hunter-Hurst

The Foundation

A spiritual coach or mentor can help you change and reshape your life by changing the way you think and operate. They can help you achieve goals change negative behaviors mindset and look deep within to fully understand the purpose God has on your life. I grew up with two parents who guided me like spiritual coaches along the way. They demonstrated in their daily lifestyle and principles and showed us how to be victorious and not victims. My dad was a pastor, and my mom a singer and minister as well. I loved church. I went to Sunday school, regular Sunday services, prayer meetings, and Bible study. We would travel all over Virginia and parts of North Carolina when my dad was asked to preach revivals. I would sit with my mom, of course, and watch my dad do what he was purposed to do – share the good news of Jesus Christ. Often when both of my parents were doing ministry, I would sometimes wonder if God would use me to sing and preach as they did.

I can remember times when my dad and mom would go to the hospital to visit the sick and pray with families. They would do weddings, baby dedications, funerals and workshops. One thing that drew me to the ministry is watching the expressions of people who were in despair or who were disappointed turn into a smile because of the compassion and spiritual guidance of my parents. Leaders and coaches always bring a message of hope in any tough situation. I knew in my teens I wanted to lead others to Jesus Christ. My parents laid the foundation of love and service to others not in just words, but through their actions. Now that I am older, I have chosen to build on the foundation that they help build.

My Life Lessons

I graduated from high school at the age of seventeen, entered college and graduated from Patrick Henry Community College in 1993. I then became engaged to be married at twenty and was married a year later. It was a very special time in my life. I landed a great job at a Fortune 500 company and purchased a nice car. I was well on my way to what I thought was the American dream. I had it all planned out – move up in management, purchase a new home and have my first child in three years – but somehow life got in the way. I always have been a huge planner, and I am very a goal-oriented person, so you might understand why the next few years took its toll on me. After about two years into my marriage, I was laid off. To make matters worse, I was having severe health problems from the stress of it all. I was determined to help my husband beat his addiction, get myself a new job, and resume my life. For years, I found myself trying to fix something that only God could correct. I became exhausted mentally and physically. I didn't understand what God was trying to teach me at the time. Honestly, I just wanted to blame him and everyone else for my troubles. I know now that wasn't the right method of thinking. In life, you should look in the mirror and not at others. In the blame game nobody wins.

After seven years of riding an emotional roller coaster, I decided I no longer wanted to ride. I wanted a new start. I relocated to another city, got a new job, and found a new church (that I rarely attended). I can remember feeling so alone, embarrassed and forgotten by everyone. A few months later, I ended up in the doctor's office where several tests were administered. I was told that I needed surgery and would have to wear a colostomy bag with little chance of child birth.

At age twenty seven, I had major surgery and remember two doctors standing over me. They said that they had "good news" and "bad news." The good news was that I didn't need a colostomy bag. The bad news was that they had to perform a complete hysterectomy because of severe endometriosis. My life had unraveled before my eyes, and all of my dreams were shattered.

While I was at the hospital, the chaplain came by to pray with me. I reluctantly smiled and said "Thank you." Then I thought a lot about Joseph in the Bible (Genesis 37). He had dreams that seemingly were sabotaged by his brothers. Joseph was put in prison, sold into slavery, and falsely accused. We would later learn it was all part of his destiny and God's plan. What I am saying is that I had some difficult situations, but it was only God's way of equipping me for the journey that I asked for at an early age. I began to muster up enough strength to walk, and following doctors' orders I moved back in with my parents. During my recovery, which lasted several months, I eventually received counseling through my job (which I hated). I was crying out of the blue for no reason, was withdrawn, and was depressed.

After a few therapy sessions, the counselor informed me of a support group called Al-Anon. I wasn't very excited about attending, but I knew I had to do something to get my life back on track. During this very difficult time I was only going to church, work and back home. I set the information on the counter in my kitchen and debated if I should give it a try. I came home one Tuesday after a rough day at work, looked at the card and made a decision to attend.

When I arrived at the facility, I felt very uncomfortable and didn't know anyone. Before the meeting started, I watched the people as a sat in my car, hugging each other, smiling and shaking hands. It took a few minutes to pull myself together, but I finally made it inside. I saw chairs in a circle, so I sat down quietly, looking down at the floor. I could feel the tears welling up inside of me. At that point, I knew I was broken. As I listened to different participants share their stories, I suddenly realized that I was not alone. As they talked about step two in the book "Courage to Change," I came to believe that a power greater than ourselves can restore our faith. I was familiar with that power but had buried it under all of life disappointments. Despair and hopelessness have a way of destroying your confidence in God. I began to regularly attend meetings and engage in conversations with the group which offered me strength and support. I personally believe that God can use non-traditional methods – like support groups – to get back on the right path in life.

My dark clouds began to slowly move away. My divorce was finalized, and I was truly on the road to healing taking it one day at a time. I found out that it really takes courage to ask for help, seek change, and humble yourself. You must forgive others and yourself so you can be free. The support group helped me focus on the things that were important. We would recite the Serenity Prayer as a reminder to "let go and let God": "God grant me the serenity to accept the things I cannot change. The courage to change the things I can and the wisdom to know the difference."

Helping Others

By my mid-thirties, my life took on a completely different turn I became a teacher and coach so I could help guide others along the way. One message I like by a popular motivational speaker is "tough times don't last but tough people do." My coaches help me see my life in a different perspective and helped me channel all my emotions into positive energy. This led me to a coaching experience I had with Lisa. I was volunteering at a organization for women, and she stayed after the group sessions to thank me for taking the time to come and help. Lisa then began to tell me about her 16-year marriage that was recently destroyed because of infidelity and how because of it her finances and home were completely destroyed. Lisa stated she was not sure how much more she could take, but her kids give her just enough hope to carry on. As I listened to Lisa, I felt led to share the few experiences I wrote about in the previous paragraphs above. She began to cry and looked amazed and said, "Really? You seem so energetic and confident." I smiled, and she apologized for crying but I wanted her to know everyone has a story but God has the divine plan for your life. I allowed circumstances just like Lisa to write chapters in my life until I realized I could not move forward by looking back. Thank God that Lisa and I are still friends to this day. She is doing well, and we often talk about how we both have grown up both spiritually and in the natural.

Conclusion

My experience coaching clients keeps me focused on my purpose and the plans God has for my life. Whether it is divorce, substance abuse, death of a loved one, or any life-changing event, what helped me was turning my life over to God and allowing Him to take the wheel and in obedience follow His lead. I believe coaches should empower, not judge, and should impart wisdom, and listen while helping individuals find their inner strength. I plan to continue to help create the life they deserve by applying simple daily principles in life that help us stay on track. Growing spiritually may challenge you to step out of your comfort zone, but your life will be deeper and stronger because of it.

Tonya Hunter-Hurst

My work in the ministry began more than 20 years ago now, when I became a licensed minister in my early 30's. Following my entrance to ministry, I obtained an Associates in Education from Patrick Henry Community College, going on to further my education at Bethlehem Bible College in 2009. I also became a certified life skills coach in 2011.

As part of my experiences, I have worked for several companies in Corporate America, where I managed groups involved in financial planning and management. From these roles, I have developed both hard and soft skills as tools that I want to pass on to others, which is my aim in the ministry. As the impartation of knowledge and wisdom, allows you to offer holistic fortification of the whole man. One method for this, is weekly messages on cable networks throughout North Carolina. I also host workshops and seminars throughout my community, to discuss topics including financial literacy, time management, and leadership.

The work I do in the ministry is a designed to bring the entire wellbeing of God's people to the forefront and ensure that each person is empowered with the tools they need to prepare for the next steps in their lives.

www.blindbutnowiseeministries.com

Architects for Health

HOW HEALTH COACHING IN THE CLINICAL SETTING HAS BECOME A POWERFUL FORCE IN TRANSFORMING HEALTHCARE

By *William K. Appelgate*

"Reaching into the 98% of healthcare that takes place outside the provider office, building individual self-care skills, prompting behavior change and accountability for health promises the greatest opportunity for transforming America's health outcomes and cost."
William K. Appelgate

True healthcare reform springs from the capacity of individuals in a population to build self-care skills, improve their health behaviors and accept accountability for health. It is about behaviors. Between 70-80 percent of healthcare costs are driven by personal behaviors. For healthcare professionals, it is not about giving motivation for behavior change, but inspiring it.

This inspiration comes more easily for some than others. Lifting health status and reducing the risks in a population can be dramatically influenced by the culture of health. However, inspiring those at most risk is the nut of achieving real clinical and cost reduction outcomes. Some individuals at higher risk will be motivated by knowledge of their condition and interest in better well-being; others will be the "drinkin, smokin, carrying-on types." Each must be reached.

The Clinical Health Coach® training was developed several

years ago by the Iowa Chronic Care Consortium specifically to drive better outcomes in population health – clinical, quality of life, patient experience and cost. It is a highly performance oriented program designed for members of a healthcare provider team. The intent is to develop a very particular set of skills to enable patients to build self-care skills, prompt improved health behaviors and inspire accountability in individuals. It was designed to address the needs of individuals requiring active care management; it serves well those benefiting from health promotion and maintenance.

This innovative training strategy was created to address three gems of evidence based knowledge: 1) 98% of healthcare takes place outside of a provider office or clinic; 2) most care is self-care, from health promotion to care of chronic conditions; and, 3) individuals and their families are the greatest underutilized resource in healthcare. This knowledge is the foundation for three breakthrough ideas for transforming healthcare.

#1. Reaching 98% of Healthcare.

Most health care takes place in the bedrooms, bathrooms and kitchens of an individual's home. In fact, seniors spend an average of only 5 hours annually (out of 8,760 in a year) in the doctor's office. Knowledgeable providers recognize that they must reach into that setting of the patient and their personal culture for best practices to be sustained and influential. Wise providers believe that they can partner with patients influencing their health behaviors and their accountability for improved outcomes. Truly competent providers know that reducing risk and improving health status for their population of patients can only be achieved by reaching into and inspiring behaviors in the 98% of healthcare.

Increasingly, healthcare has become serious about outcomes. The Triple Aim of better health, better healthcare and lower cost is more than a mere mantra for change. It is shifting our approach to healthcare and how it is paid for – from volume to value. Payors, health plans and patients are increasingly savvy regarding outcomes. Patients who have long exhibited priority interest in being "fixed" are grasping the value of reducing risk and maintaining health status. Attention to health risk and health status are longer term goals supported by improved access, prevention, timely care, management of chronic conditions and improved health behaviors.

The question is, "How can an already busy provider get to and serve all of these new interests of individuals?" And, "How can appropriate attention be given to those with the highest risk and lower health status who will experience condition exacerbations and cost?" Quite frankly, if delivered in traditional ways, they cannot. Most often it takes a healthcare team, who along with the physician can effectively partner with patients to reach into and influence what occurs in the 98% of healthcare that happens outside of the office, clinic or hospital.

#2. Recognizing the Power of Self-Care.

The Agency for Healthcare Quality and Research (AHQR) has reported that 95% of diabetes care is self-care. Even the best of physicians and healthcare providers cannot get to results by themselves. Historically, we have encouraged, sought and preferred patients who were compliant with and adherent to education, prescriptions and recommended behaviors. Those that were not were described as non-compliant or non-adherent. In truth, they were likely neither engaged nor activated.

There is a lot of talk and conversation about patient engagement. Technology is often touted as a path to engagement. Frequent contact is often recommended as a means to an engagement end. And, selected health plans and employers report that incentives prompt higher levels of engagement. These are not bad ideas. However, they miss a powerful point – engagement results most often from connecting an individual to their own expressed interests. It begins by changing the conversation from asking "What's the matter?" to "What matters to you?"

By coaching an individual to identify and claim their highest health interests – better quality of life, staying out of the hospital, remaining independent, thriving in life – the value of building self-care skills, improving health behaviors and living accountably comes alive. A patient's stated interest or goal to be around for grandchildren or travel confidently for the next several years provides powerful self-motivation for changed behavior or the practice of evidence founded self-care skills. Building self-care skills, motivation to use them and accountability to sustain health is a new high calling for all of healthcare professionals.

#3. Tapping the Great Underutilized Resource.

Telling individuals what to do, educating or warning them about the consequences of their sub-optimal health behaviors has not worked. The *New England Journal of Medicine* has reported that 30 – 50% of patients leave their provider visits without understanding their treatment plan, hospitalized patients retain only 10% of their discharge teaching instructions and chronically ill patients receive only 56% of clinically recommended health care. If this is true, it reflects reasons many patients remain a great underutilized resource.

Prior to his recent departure from his position as Director at the Office of the National Coordinator for Health Information Technology (ONC), Dr. Farsad Mostashari shared an illuminating observation, "We are in an era of looking at all of the underutilized resources in healthcare. The greatest underutilized resource in healthcare is the patient and their families. The next big healthcare application will be behavioral informatics—how do we understand behavioral change, not just give people knowledge, but helping people tap into their rationality."

Tapping into patients and their families utilizing them as a resource requires knowledge about a patient's interests and rationality. In the 1960s, a traditional healthcare encounter was physician centered and self-executed. The elements were: gather information; perform examination; offer diagnosis; and, give instructions. Today, effective encounters are collaborative, patient centered and team executed. The elements include: open discussion; build relationship; gather information; understand patient perspective; perform examination; share information; determine patient interest in change; agree on problem and plan; provide closure; and, plan follow-up.

Personal Accountability Imperative

Dr. Toby Cosgrove, CEO of Cleveland Clinic, appearing on Meet the Press, was asked, "What is the one big breakthrough opportunity we have to change the nature of healthcare in this country?" He did not talk legislation and funding. Instead, he observed that the biggest challenge, and opportunity, for the future of healthcare is getting people to take greater personal responsibility for their own health.

Reaching effectively into the 98% of care, believing in health behavior change and inspiring it, and partnering with the patient to tap this great underutilized resource represents a departure from, "how we have always done it." Healthcare professionals must move from "do, teach, tell" to "ask, listen, inspire." Rather than focusing service on the origin and treatment of disease, they focus upon the maintenance and development of health. In short, the effective healthcare provider is a designer and builder of health – an architect for health.

To effectively partner with patients in the new design and build of health, healthcare professionals must be skilled in transforming the conversation between themselves and patients they serve. They must be behavior change specialists, not seeing the end of their work as teaching or telling a patient the best steps to care, but growing the patient's ability and confidence in long lasting behavior change. A patient labeled "non-compliant" is often someone who needs further exploration in discovering their own motivation for change. These healthcare professionals must also be attentive to population health processes, acting as care facilitators who align best practice care with patient centered resources.

An analogy can be drawn between what therapists do in working with patients and what coaches do. Therapists often look back at the causes and background of individuals as a source of what causes the present situation – they act as an archeologist. In contrast, a coach picks-up an individual where they are and acts to design or create a new or better future – they act as an architect.

Health coaching is fundament to delivering true patient-centered care. While this can be challenging for a healthcare team, there are powerful health coach techniques and strategies that will complement the care team's clinical expertise delivering a new level of patient engagement and activation. Health coaching strategies improve the entire team. Coaching skills enable physicians, care coordinators, community health workers, ANPs, PAs, dietitians, social workers and other healthcare professionals to move behaviors. Our mission in the Clinical Health Coach® training is building highly competent, performance oriented individuals who can truly become architects for health! Who could ask for a higher calling?

Meet William K. Appelgate

William K. Appelgate believes that inspiring improved personal health behaviors is the change-the-world strategy required for the future of healthcare in America. He is the Executive Director of the Iowa Chronic Care Consortium and Founder of the Clinical Health Coach® training. His professional work has included service as a director of a university research center, a college foundation director, a college president, C.E.O. of two comprehensive, innovative healthcare systems as well as vice-president and clinical professor at a leading graduate health sciences university and medical school.

The Iowa Chronic Care Consortium, along with the Clinical Health Coach®, is a non-profit population health capacity building organization with clients and trainees in 45 states. It has received national recognition for its particular skill in achieving dramatic validated clinical and cost outcomes through prompting health behavior change in patient populations.

Dr. Appelgate earned a B.S. from Iowa State University, an M.A. from Loyola University of Chicago and a Ph.D. from Southern Illinois University. He is a Vietnam Era Veteran and a Certified Professional Coach.

To learn more about health coaching in the clinical setting – the innovation healthcare really needs – visit www.clinicalhealthcoach.com. To immediately access valuable insight, webinars and resources on this breakthrough strategy, join the free Clinical Health Coach® Learning Community at http://clinicalhealthcoach.com/learningcommunity/ Receive a free ebook on coaching in the clinical setting here: http://clinicalhealthcoach.com/architects-signup

Regain Health through Mind, Body, Spirit Coaching

Standing in Agreement with the Client's Dream of Health

By Debra Simon

"Medical doctors look at the body NOT the driving spirit." ~ Debra Simon

---

Welcome to the world of Mind, Body, Spirit Coaching offered at Love Energy Medicine, Inc. Here you will find that every aspect of who you are is not just appreciated, but honored, heard and supported. Together, we will help you to relax the mind just a bit so that the heart and every aspect of who you are, has a voice.

Get to know your coach. Debra Simon, Energy Medicine Practitioner, Healing Touch Certified Practitioner and Certified Professional Coach will stand in agreement with your dream of wellness. Learning a little about Debra's path will help you to appreciate why she is so passionate about her mission.

Debra's story:

I learned early in life that there are house rules that must be followed. People older than you are wiser. Those with more education are the experts. "Do as you're told" is the key to success. This training did not bode well for what was to come. Perhaps, it created what was to come to help awaken my spirit, gifts, and purpose.

In my 20's, I was working at a prestigious medical school. Working in development, I reported to the dean of the school. My husband was an internal medicine specialist. There I was, surrounded by traditional medicine and my health was declining.

For years, I followed the old house rules. My mind went into a fog. I took the prescription drugs without question. The world seemed to be falling apart. The prescriptions worked and then the symptoms got louder. Prescription dosages were increased and periodically changed. I felt hopeless, disempowered, broken while trying to keep up with the demands of my job. My challenging relationship broke into a million pieces and we divorced.

After years of bullying my mind, body and spirit, the final blow came. I was told, "You will either die or soon we will have to remove your colon." My doctors used the words, "no known cause and no known cure." I was handed brochures to explain the procedures. My heart sank. I felt broken. Why was my body abandoning my will? My heart would not let me proceed with the surgery. I went against the advice and pressure from my doctors and my family. My intention was to find another way. I was willing to die in the pursuit of wellness. I don't recommend that others follow this example as the results may very well turn out differently. I simply share my story to encourage and empower preventive action while there is still time for course adjustments.

FIVE points of awareness that saved my life:

Medical doctors look at the body NOT the driving spirit. Their tools are medicine and surgery. They're often not interested in the "Why" behind the symptoms.

Symptoms are the language of the body. The body is so magnificently created that with the voice of symptoms, it can guide you to physical wellness. Before the physical wellness arrives, the journey will often guide a person to discover personal power and purpose.

The value of who we are is eternal. You can take a $100 bill and drop it in the mud. You can run over it with a tank and push it so deep into the mud that it can no longer be seen. Earth may cover it, but human actions will not change the value.

Obstacles cut the diamond. We each are presented with life challenges. The rich are not exempt. Challenges may bring new awareness. Utilizing the mind, body and spirit to work through the obstacles can produce the precise cuts to create a beautiful diamond.

The heart knows the way. If we can't force ourselves to do something, it may very well be that the heart is preventing a misstep. Explore the hesitation.

In the pursuit of wellness, parts of me did die. The part of me that had been trained by the world and my culture died a slow and painful death. My illness chiseled a new creation and motivated me to reclaim my power and my voice. I now see that symptoms are an amazing language of the body and spirit. The body knows how to reveal our eternal light. The obstacles provide the precise cuts to bring us home. When we shine the light on our truth, the heart will lead the way.

When we hear the words, "no known cause and no known cure" we may be at the brink of an exhilarating self-discovery. This is not the end. This is the beginning. The diagnosis may be where traditional medicine drops us off and where Mind, Body, Spirit Coaching begins.

We don't have to wait until things get dire. We can begin today to listen and empower Mind, Body and Spirit.

Here are the tools I use...

Empowering the mind happens through coaching conversation. We begin by giving you an opportunity to share where you've been and what you believe to be true. You are empowered to speak about your dream for your life. The stories of your life are important. Your unique experiences are coming together to create your exact NOW. I will stand in agreement with your dream of wellness. I am not a licensed medical provider so I will ask that your medical providers track your progress. I'm part of the team. Each session is a full two hour experience. The coaching conversation allows us time to set the short term goal and the long term goal of working together.

Empowering the body and spirit happens through the Energy Medicine experience. We have just spoken the goal. The body and spirit have heard the conversation. My gift is to coach the mind into a greater body and spirit awareness. Recognizing the biofield as part of the body and spirit, we gain access to information previously unavailable.

At this point, you may be asking, "What is the biofield and what is energy medicine?" Let's fill in the gaps. In 1992, the National Institute of Health coined the term "biofield" to describe the information rich field that surrounds the human body. They determined that adjustments in the biofield are beneficial. Interestingly, this was happening in the same year my doctors were using the terms "no known cause and no known cure" for the symptoms in my body. Many people are familiar with the 7 main energy centers of the body. These are the doors to the rich information in the biofield.

Shortly after my health returned more than 20 years ago, I began to feel the biofield that surrounds each person. My hands read the biofield similar to the way a blind person reads braille. My hands are the instruments. As with any skill, experience matters. When I began doing the work, the field of energy medicine had not developed so I became a massage therapist but everyone who arrived was seeking my gift of reading the energy system of the body.

Later, I became a Healing Touch Certified Practitioner. This is currently the only accredited energy medicine training in the United States. The accrediting body is the National Commission for Certifying Agencies (NCCA). They accredit over 300 professions including the National Commission of Certification of Physician Assistants. This accrediting body is considered the gold standard. My gift is to apply the techniques with precision while responding to the fluctuations in the body's magnificent and mostly invisible biofield.

Through Mind, Body, Spirit Coaching my clients have benefited. I stand in agreement with the client's goal. They are the authority. I don't speak about what's possible or not possible. The truth is that each person brings their own miracle. My understandings of what's possible has expanded over the past 20 years. Common experiences are laughter followed by, "This is amazing! I didn't know that was possible! I never knew that about myself!" I facilitate the process and provide a safe place to excavate the true self by giving voice to each dynamic part: Mind, Body and Spirit.

Some client experiences:

1. He endured a steel beam going through his foot behind his steel toe work boot. Following the surgeries, bone formed and he was able to walk. The pain persisted for more than 18 years. Today, he successfully manages a business and is able to walk and stand without pain.
2. She was diagnosed with cancer and wanting pain management. During our time together, she began chemotherapy. After several sessions she discovered that her greatest fear was that she would live. We used this opportunity to unravel the fear and find resources to help her. Her cancer resolved.
3. The trauma of her childhood had prevented her from knowing her true identity. She discovered that her eternal light was bright. Her gifts became known and she began to take positive and empowered action to create a life of freedom.
4. Following a multi-vehicle pileup, she had been seeing nine pain management doctors per week. The proposed surgeries offered no assurance of recovery. The risks were great. Her doctors agreed to give her time to make some important decisions. We began the journey while time was still on our side. Within a few sessions she noticed that the pain was subsiding. Her medical doctors continued to monitor her progress and encouraged her to continue with the new modality producing positive results. She not only healed, but she returned to her family as a caregiver during her father's remaining months of life.

D ebra Simon, Energy Medicine Practitioner, Healing Touch Certified Practitioner and Certified Professional Coach is the owner of Love Energy Medicine, Inc. She is a member of the Healing Touch Professional Association and Business Network International.

She was working at a prestigious medical school and married to a medical doctor when her health began to fail. She was surrounded by traditional medicine; yet, the prescriptions and treatments were not restoring her health. She decided to explore other options and found the power of healing through the energy system of the body. With more than 20 years of experience, she offers Mind, Body, Spirit Coaching utilizing conversation and her unique gift to read the biofield. Clients release congested energies and false self-image. A vibrant life is born.

LEARN HOW ENERGY MEDICINE CAN PROVIDE GREAT RESULTS AND SUPPORT FOR THE FOLLOWING AND MORE…

Stress Management, Sleep Issues, Adult ADD, Depression, Grief & loss, Heart Issues, Traumatic Events, Pain Relief,

Concussion Symptom Relief, Living with Cancer

Email <u>DebraSimonHealthCoach@gmail.com</u> or call 1-888-448-3486

Your questions answered: Enjoy a complimentary 30 Minute Phone Consultation.

Reserve a seat: *Introduction to Energy Medicine Class*.

Two Hour Healing Experience.

Clients living outside the Denver, Colorado area arrive by plane, train and automobile.

Live Your Dream!

What Are You Working So Hard For?
By Doug Jarvie

I decided to retire when I had enough: enough of people telling me when I could have my vacation and how long it could be, and enough money to finance the travel I wanted to do. When asked why I was retiring, I replied, "If I don't tell you, you will make up more interesting stories than my real reason." The story I told myself was that my time was worth more to me than others were willing to pay for it. Having the power to control my own time and what I do with it is priceless. Now I am free to volunteer my time as much or as little as I choose and to schedule it around the time I choose to travel.

I recommend travelling and enjoying something while you still have the health, strength, and stamina to do so. It is not so much about what you are retiring from, but what you are retiring to. Barbara, through Wainwright Global, taught me about life coaching. The first lesson was about asking questions. Listening to the answers was lesson two. Here are nine questions worth asking yourself:

1. Is there something you would rather be doing than what you're doing right now?
2. Are you having fun yet?
3. Do you take time to have enough rest, to relax, restore, and replenish yourself? Remember you cannot deliver from an empty well.
4. Do you reward yourself for your accomplishments?
5. Do you spend more time planning a two-week vacation than you spend planning for a twenty-year retirement?
6. How much longer will you have to keep working so hard?
7. Do you plan to retire, or do you plan to work until you drop?
8. How much money do you need to retire?

9. Where do you want to retire to? Will you live in the same place or move to another city or another country? Maybe you will live on a boat and cruise around the world.

If you are just starting a coaching business, build your business with the exit plan in mind. Do not think of it as a plan to get out when things get bad, but a plan to get out when things get good. Plan to build a successful business that is attractive to buyers.

The simplest exit strategy may be to increase your personal salary or take bonuses in the final years before finally closing the doors. After closing the doors, the assets can be liquidated, and any debts paid off. This method will probably incur the largest income tax penalty.

Perhaps you want to build a company with a partner and create a plan for selling your shares in the company to your partners when you want to leave. Consider spreading the payment, and related tax burden out over several years.[1]

Another popular exit strategy is to sell the company to another corporation or individual who is interested in continuing what you have built. You may negotiate to stay on as an advisor for a few years or months and receive dividends or a salary. Perhaps you know of a competitor who is looking to expand their business and may be interested in your contacts and customers. You may even be able to acquire equity in the new company as part of the sale valuation.

In the 1980s, the London Life Insurance Company promoted early retirement with an ad called Freedom 55.[2] In today's reality, promoting Freedom 55 and the idea of advertising early retirement is passé. At that time, when interest rates were approaching eight percent, $1.5 million was required to retire and interest would provide all living expenses and growth for inflation. Now ads ask, "What does your freedom look like?" and they are trying to sell to an audience who is thinking of retiring at the age of 71 years. (As a rule of thumb, the cost of living doubles every ten years.)

Here are a few examples of how people have retired.

1. George, like many who reach their 50s in the corporate world, became culled from the herd by "rightsizing." Imagine a rectangular-shaped working cohort on their way up the ladder of success, finding the ladder getting narrower as they climb into the triangular-shaped management structure. George, like others faced by this situation, became a consultant. He became his own employer and hired himself, so he would not be out of work. As a consultant, he took on work for previous clients, contacts, and employers when they had projects with critical delivery dates and did not have enough staff to fulfill the requirements. They called George in when they had critical situations caused by their own delays. One time when George was expecting a visit from his son and grandchildren he received such a call. It was for a critical project with only ten days to complete it. George was faced with the choice between spending time with his grandchildren or working on the project. George chose precious family time.
2. Another catalyst for planning to retire begins when there is a change of ownership in a company you have been working in for many years. Here is what happened to Robert when he was faced with this situation. First, he noticed that the new business model did not mesh well with the old methods. Some employees were offered a retirement package and others were left waiting, anticipating a package. Some could not wait any longer and retired early, a few years before retirement plans could begin paying out. When Robert chose early retirement, he was much happier. He and his wife became more active in their local church and community. They were able to travel internationally to special church-related functions around the world.
3. Norman's retirement plan came about because of personal family turmoil. His job required concentration which was no longer possible, as he was distracted by his personal family problems. Looking back, he says it was like receiving a "get out of jail free card." He is enjoying retirement despite having

some health problems. Norman told me that research has shown that those who retire early live a longer life than those who stay in a demanding job.

How do I like to spend my retirement? I like to travel to see how life is evolving in other parts of the world. I recommend you do this while the mind and body are still capable. I travel often, and I prefer cruise ships to get me from country to country. It is a great way to see many of the world's port cities. Land excursions are available where bus and train transportation whisk us away to the inland sites. On more than a few of these cruises, I have chosen an extended excursion which requires several days off the ship, and air flights into the interior of the country. The most recent adventure was a visit to the Taj Mahal in north-central India. We left the ship in the port city of Cochin and travelled by bus to the airport where we caught an airplane to the city of Delhi. After an overnight stay in a world-class hotel, we boarded a local train, the Gatimaan Express, and travelled to the northern city of Agra.

The Taj Mahal is beautiful, and I was even more intrigued by the nearby Agra Fort. It is also known as the Red Fort because of the red sandstone used to build it. Instead of a train ride back to Delhi, we travelled by bus through the agricultural areas of India. The smell of smoke permeated the bus because farmers were burning stalks from last year's crops. The spacious hotel was a welcome escape from the crowds. In the morning, we had a bumpy rickshaw ride over the cobblestones of the old part of Delhi. In the afternoon, we took a flight from Delhi to Mumbai. A quick bus tour of Mumbai brought us back to the ship which had sailed on from Cochin.

I am using this example to show how travelling can open all our senses to wonderful things. Don't wait, do this while you are in good physical health. Although the hotels are wheelchair accessible, many of the ancient sites such as Angkor Wat in Cambodia, Petra in Jordan, or Machu Picchu in Peru are not as easily accessed.

I have seen passengers with walkers and wheelchairs moving up and down the gangways. Some ports are not directly accessible by ship and tenders are used to transport passengers to shore. A tender could be considered a water bus and are definitely not a luxury tour bus; they are more like a school bus. They are fitted with hard fiberglass seats, and plastic doors that roll up and occasionally allow the rough seas to blow in. On a calm day, it is a way to the beach. When the weather changes, it can be a white-knuckle roller coaster ride up and down the waves back to the ship. These are the things that can change a vacation into an adventure.

What can you draw from this? Travelling with a physical disability is possible and worth the extra effort. At one port I watched a passenger use her own Segway to travel around the beautiful grounds of the largest Buddhist Fokuangshan monastery in Taiwan. Follow this link to my travel blog to see a couple of pictures of the monastery and many other places. https://jarvie.ca/kaohsiung-stadium

Where do you want to go today?

References:

1. Daniel Richards, *Writing a Business Plan: Creating a Business Exit Plan* (May 31, 2017), https://www.thebalance.com/writing-a-business-plan-planning-your-exit-strategy-1200841
2. Susan Krashinsky, *Reality check for Freedom 55* (March 26, 2017), https://www.theglobeandmail.com/report-on-business/industry-news/marketing/reality-check-for-freedom-55/article4523976/

Doug Jarvie

Doug has been retired since 2007 and is enjoying travelling and photographing this wonderful world. In his blog, Doug shares pictures of the places he has visited, provides a little information about these unique places, and hopes to inspire others to travel and appreciate the variety of life around us. When at home, Doug volunteers as a sound technician and uses his coaching training as a lay pastoral visitor, and a friend in a community outreach program.

Since high school, Doug has been an ongoing learner, and teacher. After graduating from DeVry University in Electronic Engineering Technology, he taught electronics and related math and science courses. Still hungry to learn, Doug completed an Honours Bachelor of Science degree in Physics at the University of Waterloo. He has managed the production, delivery, and repair of electronic devices, designed and programmed microprocessor control systems, and managed the engineering of supervisory control and data acquisition (SCADA) systems.

In retirement, he is studying French and Spanish for fun.

Check out and enjoy pictures of Doug's travel adventures on his web site: https://jarvie.ca

The Importance of an Academic Life Coach

HOW I EMPOWER AND MAKE A DIFFERENCE
By Dawn A. Peters-Bascombe

"Many young people fail to achieve their career milestones because no one prepares them for the road ahead." Dawn A. Peters-Bascombe

Introduction

What is Academic Life Coaching?

According to Williams (2017), Academic Life Coaching is a program that is intended to help students thrive and develop positive life skills. It goes beyond youth mentoring and counseling by helping students understand how to learn best at school, be proactive, and exercise personal leadership. When students learn these skills, they are able to avoid common pitfalls and can significantly influence the upward path of personal fulfillment and success.

Jane's Story on Academic Life Coaching

Most young people find it difficult to make career decisions, and Jane, a 25-year-old college student, was no different. Four years ago, Jane approached me, an academic life coach, and asked, "When did you know that you made the right career choice?" Jane was in her first year of the undergraduate law program at a southern Ontario university in Canada. Right out of high school Jane was accepted into a science program to complete her undergraduate prerequisite for medical school. However, Jane completed one year of the science program and then switched her major.

The following year, Jane was accepted into the Information Technology (IT) program because she felt that law was not her calling, but six months into the program she dropped out. She felt that she was more of a people's person and wanted to choose a profession where she could make a difference. When I met Jane, she was not sure if she made the right decision to take the law program. She was struggling to keep up with assignments and readings but felt that she was doing her best. Jane was worried that one failing grade would put her below the acceptable passing grade point average to remain in the program. Jane and her parents requested that I provide some direction for Jane by becoming her academic life coach. Many young people lack guidance and direction during the career decision making process, and spend the early part of their young adulthood in confusion.

Barriers to Success

Being a first generation Canadian

Jane was a first generation Canadian whose parents emigrated from Brazil many years ago. She had three younger sisters whose ages were 17, 12, and 10. Jane stated that there was a lot of pressure on her from every corner in her family because she was the first person in her family to attend a university. She believed that everyone expected her to succeed. At that point in her life, Jane felt that she was destined to fail. Jane was in a dilemma. She entered university at first with a major influenced by her parents. She soon realized that her career choice did not fit with her own identity. Jane was trying to live up to the dreams of her parents.

Too many options to choose from

According to Yates (2013), some individuals have more options than others to choose from. The author believes that the amount of career options one has is determined by several factors, such as his or her personality, abilities, qualification, location, class, ethnicity, gender, age, health, economic climate, role model, luck, attitudes, and family background. Yates stated that some young people may feel that their career path is related to the circumstances in their lives and to a degree are pre-destined because of their geography and their socioeconomic status. Having too many career options to choose from added to Jane's confusion and made things very difficult to stick to one career path. As an academic life coach, I entered into Jane's life and helped her with her decision making and career exploration.

Career Exploration

According to Gillie and Gillie-Isenhour (2003), career exploration opens up the horizons and opens up students' minds to a whole world they did not know existed; it gives a reality check and helps students to find answers to basic and important questions in regard to money and competitive careers fields; it creates a realistic action plan to get young people where they want to go; it saves time and money by helping the individual to discover a career interest early on and help them to identify educational options that will support their future; and it helps to build self-confidence and helps to motivate them to achieve their goals and higher grades, and to feel better prepared for the future. Jane decided to remain with the undergraduate law program and I supported her. However, she would have benefited better from an academic life coach while still in high school.

A roller coaster ride without an academic life coach

During Jane's early college program exploration she experienced a roller coaster ride in her decision making process. The coach would have provided Jane with the opportunity to choose the college program that was best suited to her. He or she could have helped Jane to develop self-confidence, a positive mindset, and a sense of control over the decision making process. Jane could have gained a deeper understanding of how to choose a program with the best fit for her emerging identity. At the time, since Jane decided to stay in the undergraduate law program, my job was to help Jane develop self-discipline and provide the help that she needed to succeed. By listening attentively to Jane, I was able to help her set realistic goals. Locke and Latham (2002) believed that "setting personal goals, which entailed commitment and self-efficiency, were the most immediate, conscious motivational determinants of actions" (p. 709).

Benefit of an academic life coach

Bimrose, Hughes, and Barnes (2011) stated that all of us will be involved in career decisions at some point in time, and the authors believed that those who work with a career coach tend to make better decisions. As an academic life coach, I helped Jane to discover her inner feelings about the best approach moving forward. Greenwood (2008) believed that a person will more likely put plans into action subsequent to career support, and will also tend to report higher levels of satisfaction with his or her career choices. I had the opportunity to help Jane build a good foundation in regard to self-empowerment, self-development, self-confidence, self-esteem, and self-efficacy.

Coaching and Empowerment

As an academic coach, I am possessed with an empowerment attitude and beliefs that were needed to sustain and support Jane. Curtis (2008) stated that one way to look at the side-by-side nature of youth empowerment is to view it as a three-legged seat. She believes that each leg of the seat represents a vital aspect of true empowerment. The first leg of the empowerment model focuses on opportunity, the second leg focuses on skills, and the final leg represents trust. Curtis believes that trust takes the longest to achieve. It was important for Jane to trust me as her academic life coach. Jane is set to graduate in June 2018. Jane's ability to work with a coach provided that opportunity to start the empowerment process.

When I first met Jane, she lacked motivation, confidence,

organization, and strategies to apply various skills to succeed in her law program. I provided strategies to promote effective study habits and skills, to enhance communication skills, note taking skills, and to learn how to trouble shoot the learning process. Within the first year of coaching Jane was more: self-sufficient, self-directed, assertive, and she was getting the work done. The feedback from her professors was positive and Jane expressed her confidence about her work. Many students were not given the same opportunity, so they struggled throughout the entire process and experience.

Conclusion

I listened to what Jane was saying and helped her to identify her strengths and weaknesses. According to Meissner (2000), listening is not the same as hearing. He believes that listening is done with the mind rather than just the ears. Most young individuals want to leave college with skills that assist them to find a good job, but they also want to enjoy their time while being there. They want to meet friends, have companionship, romances, and enjoy party going. They want to do the things that all young adults find pleasurable as a part of growing up. However, for them to accomplish this, they need the help to balance their college work and play. With good academic and personal planning they can experience career advantage and personal growth and satisfaction. Now, can you see how an academic life coach can help you and your family?

References

Bimrose, J., Hughes, D., & Barnes, S. A. (2011). *Integrating new technologies into careers practice: Extending the knowledge base.* London: UK Commission for Employment and Skills.

Curtis, K. (2008). *Empowering youth: How to encourage young leaders to do great things.* Minneapolis, MN: Search Institute.

Gillie, S., & Gillie-Isenhour, M. (2003). The educational, social, and economic value of informed and considered career decisions.

America's career Resource Network Association. Retrieved from http://www.bridges.com/us/training/resnwhitepapers/ACRN_ICCD.pdf

Greenwood, J. I. (2008). Validation of a multivariate career and educational counseling intervention model using long term follow up. *Career Development Quarterly, 56*(4), 353-361. doi: 10.1002/j.2161-0045.2008.tb00100.x

Locke, E., & Latham, G. (2002). Building a practical useful theory of goal setting and task motivation. *American Psychologist, 3*(7), 705-717.

Meissner, W. W. (2000). On analytic listening. *Psychoanalytic Quarterly, 6* (2), 317-367. Retrieved from https://www.tandfonline.com/doi/abs/10.1002/j.2167-4086.2000.tb00565.x?journalCode=upaq20

Williams, J. A. (2017). Academic life coach training program. Retrieved from https://www.johnandrewwilliams.com/

Yates, J. (2013). *The career coaching handbook*. New York, NY: Taylor and Francis Group.

Dr. Dawn Peters-Bascombe

Professional Background

Dr. Peters-Bascombe, a Certified Professional Coach, is a nurse educator with Ryerson University and George Brown College in Ontario, Canada. She is a high-performing healthcare professional with many years of experience in the fields of Nursing, Management, and Education.

Education and Experience

Dr. Peters-Bascombe holds a Bachelor of Science in Nursing from Ryerson University, Ontario, Canada; a Master of Science in Nursing, and a Doctor of Education and Health Policy from D'Youville College, New York, U.S.A. Dr. Peters-Bascombe has worked with several prestigious healthcare institutions in Canada and the United States and has coached clients, students, and members of various communities.

Personal Details

Dr. Peters-Bascombe, born in St. Vincent and the Grenadines, currently resides in Ontario, Canada with her children. She gained insight into a purpose-filled life five years ago, and since that time she vowed to spend her life empowering others to solve life problems and to become the best that they can be. In this book, the Power of Coaching, Dr. Peters-Bascombe stated that many young people fail to achieve their career milestones because no one prepares them for the road ahead. Dr. Peters-Bascombe can be reached at dawnpeters07@yahoo.com.

Stay Present. Live in the Now

Every Thought is a Gift
By Paul Sahota

"True power is being present in your thoughts. Choose your thoughts, wisely." ~ Paul Sahota

---

My life began in a remote village in northern India. My father left for Canada when I was one, returning seven years later to bring us to Canada. With no memory of my father; I had no idea who the sharply dressed man was standing in the schoolyard one day while I was getting the stick from the teacher across my backside. Why? Because I could not remember all the twelve times tables at the age of eight! Even in India, the school system was based on memory skills, not thought. I wanted my dad to be proud of me and yet, at that moment, I only have a vivid memory of feeling shame and embarrassment. When I found out we would be moving from the only life that I knew I ran and hid in a mango tree and ate ripe mangoes. I feared change, and I had also developed a severe case of the runs from eating so many mangoes! I recall my mother thinking on her feet as to how to send in an acceptable stool sample for the medical test needed for me to enter Canada. She split my brother's sample into two and sent them off to the lab. I wondered how could she do this? How was that being honest? In my life I have had many teachers and mentors, the right ones taught me to lead by example; to do as they do. Through keeping an open mind and learning from the experiences of others, I realize it was best not to do as they do. I love and respect my parents; they are my first teachers. As it turned out, my brother's sample failed and mine passed.

Enroute to Canada we had a long layover in Hong Kong airport. Tired and hungry, not being able to speak English or Chinese, we sat in a room with sliding glass doors. Through the glass we could see 5 or 6 full-length tables set up with food; it looked foreign and delicious. My parents were afraid to leave the waiting area in case we missed our connection, so we sat there watching people eat. Later we learned that that banquet of food was meant for us as well. I realize now when looking back how many times in my life an opportunity was right there in front of me and I just had to step through that door and claim it. Sometimes all I needed to do was speak up and ask.

In Canada, I was moved back two years in school because I did not know any English at the time. As a child, this was devastating. I thought I was not smart enough, yet in math, I excelled ahead of my peers.

Have you ever felt that because of your circumstances you were not smart enough? Not beautiful, not worthy, not loveable, or deserving? Have you ever thought "I am not enough, I was not born in the correct time, place or country?" "If only I was taller, spoke a different language, was a different skin color." Are you living in fear, fear of rejection, fear of failure, fear of success? "Something is wrong with me. Why me?" I thought or said all of those to myself.

I always thought my situation was unique and nobody was experiencing the same thing. I didn't have anyone to open up to, that could relate to my situation. When I tried to speak to my parents they did not know how to help me, nor believe my story. Can you relate?

Where did those thoughts and feelings come from? I was not born with any of those. Yet I felt so insignificant, I could not communicate clearly, so I would withdraw from conversations. I finally found my sanctuary in sports; I only needed to listen to the coach's direction and let my actions do the talking. I would push my body to compete in soccer, basketball, football, baseball, etc. I thought my popularity was tied to my sports ability.

After high school I trained in Martial arts, traveling to Japan to get my Brown belt in Kyokushin Karate. One of my greatest honors was to meet Mr. Mas Oyama, the founder of this great art. I was training to get my black belt when a drunk driver ended that vision for me; I was lucky to be alive when they pulled me from my car.

I worked many jobs after school and weekends to help my family. At the age of 14, I got a job and my first mentor, a local automotive business owner. After five weeks of seeing him every Saturday morning as he arrived to open his shop; he jokingly said, "You are more reliable than my employees by showing up every week to ask for a job". I replied, "The best decision you could make today is to hire me!" After a brief second of deliberation and thought on his part, he said, "Grab a broom and sweep the floor". My persistence paid off!

Reflecting, this was a profound experience for me as at that age; I had no idea where those words came from, they just popped out of my mouth.

I have heard many times that I am an old soul from many people growing up; this was one of those times when I intuitively said what came to me from the source. Over the years of growing up, experiencing life, school, marriage, becoming a father, personally developing myself and in coaching others - I have grown to trust my own intuition.

I earned my way up to sales manager, in charge of my own automotive store. This is where having a vision is most important; I had the leadership role of increasing sales and profits. My old paradigm told me that success could only be accomplished through hard work; to this day that programming still is my blessing and my curse. I realize now that thoughts become things.

Even still, I had many layers of deeply-rooted beliefs that held me back.

When I was introduced to personal development and coaching in 1996, I began letting go of many of these limiting beliefs, continuing to release them to this day. I began to feel freer in many aspects of my life. I learned to communicate better both in my listening and speaking. I learned that I have about 60 thousand thoughts per day, and that many of these thoughts are the same as the day before. Not every thought is positive, yet I realize now that I have the power to control and choose my own thoughts by being present in each moment. I can choose an empowering belief or a disempowering one.

The power is in my choice of thoughts. To make anything happen, I have learned to stay present as much as possible in every precious second, letting the minutes and the hours take care of themselves. I have learned to do this through active guided meditation.

I had been taught that I must work long and hard for my money. That money doesn't grow on trees, and to save my money for a rainy day. I grew up with many limiting beliefs about money and other things. Can you relate? Abundance is my birthright. I was not meant to live with stress or a scarcity consciousness. Through the power of coaching and learning, I have come to understand that there is only abundance - there is no lack, no limitations. I now take time to look around for myself and appreciate the abundance of nature. Where miracles occur every day, nature does not lack anything. The source is unlimited, and I am no different from anyone else; we are all connected to the same source. How could tapping into the source enrich your life?

Money is energy, and like air, there is an unlimited supply and there will always be more than enough for me, my family, and for everyone.

The power lies in my thoughts and my feelings. Thoughts create images, images create feelings and emotions, feelings create beliefs, beliefs create actions, and actions create results. I choose my thoughts wisely.

I assist people in becoming present in their thoughts, to have the life they perhaps have only dreamt of or have maybe even given up on. I kept a scorecard to tally my positive versus negative thoughts throughout each day for a week. The side scoring the highest will come into my reality. I challenge you to keep a scorecard for one week to track your predominant thought patterns. Visit my website to download your free scorecard.

Choosing my own thoughts and having a clear vision without limitations is the most empowering place I can possibly choose to live my life from. Every thought is neutral; people are not. My purpose is to help you make this your truth. I would be honored to help guide you toward achieving this now. Learn to calm your mind so you can control your thoughts. Self-guided or active-guided meditation helps you to quickly and easily make the necessary changes to be in control of your own thoughts.

My three main learnings from coaching are:

Let go of my past.
Stay present in each moment
Dream big.

What is possible when you think positive thoughts for yourself? Will you track your thoughts for a minimum of 24 hours, keeping score of positive versus negative thoughts?

Get started now with my FREE guided abundance meditation: www.CoachPaulSahota.com

Paul Sahota is a committed, powerful, compassionate leader with a life devoted to inspiring others to reach their goals, have a purpose, and live their dreams. Paul has coached for over 20 years. We each have our own unique "Master Key"; allow Paul to help you unlock your mind. Paul is an author, speaker, Certified Professional Coach (through Wainwright Global) and a Certified Silva UltraMind ESP Instructor. Paul worked in the auto industry for 37 years. He has over 20 years in the Personal Development industry, as well as coaching, training, and sales. Paul was a Director of a nonprofit foundation for over 12 years, helping children around the world through many projects. He is also a Real Estate Investor.

Paul Sahota was born in northern India, traveled to Canada in 1968 to meet his soul mate, Tanya. Their inter racial marriage in 1985 brought different cultures and religions together, they are blessed with a son and a daughter. They live near Vancouver, BC Canada.

Without a vision, the people perish. I invite you to join me, so we can leave this planet in a better place.

Paul has coached many people to create liberty in their personal and professional lives. www.PaulSahota.com email: coachsahota@gmail.com

Igniting the Inner Coach, Light Body to Awaken Self

By Susmita Barua

"When you tap into your intuitive and embodied feminine wisdom, you unlock your code to live with enlightened purpose, passion, joy and creative freedom." ~ Susmita Barua

---

Do we have an inner guide, silent witness, observer, or intuitive knowing voice within us that we can tap into in times of pain and struggle? I believe we all do. Yet not everyone recognizes or develops trust in it. I was aware of this witnessing presence from early childhood. The earliest memory of my childhood dream was something like a falling feather through a spiraling loop to wake up on this earth plane. My first shocking thought about the fall was, 'have I sinned?' The next thought was, wait I am born a Buddhist and not a Christian! I could hardly know what Buddhism or Christianity was in my little child brain. Yet there was a knowing or some kind of memory within me. I recall while in kindergarten I would ponder and evaluate the ethics of an action by my teacher as it was unfolding. Sometime I would directly perceive the import and depth of one single moment or event as culmination of many previous moments. One time in the middle of the very intensely joyful moment of playing hide and seek, when all my friends disappeared to hide, and I was left alone to seek them, I had this thought. "Why is this game so much fun for us?" Instantly an answer came from the expanded awareness, because no one is actually lost or hidden for good, eventually we find each other. Are children born with a blank slate without memory or mental content (tabula rasa)? My experience tells me otherwise.

I grew up in a tiny minority Bengali Buddhist community in Calcutta (now Kolkata). Around age ten I received my first big birthday gift from my father's friend. Reading this 'Children's Book of Knowledge' filled me with great excitement and wonder. I had a conversation within me about Einstein and Buddha, who to follow as my role model in education? Without knowing much anything about them I felt they were both seeking the same goal about nature of reality, unified field, universal truth from two different frames of mind one focused inward (Buddha) and one focused outward into the material world. The next question was, "how would Buddha know the ultimate Truth without help of science, math and technology?" Then in the form of a whisper came another question, "what if this human mind-body is a divine instrument capable of sensing, realizing and awakening to the ultimate Truth?" Anyway Buddha's kind face of wisdom and compassion for all beings to end suffering by ending ignorance attracted me more. It seemed more appropriate for living with inner peace, harmony and happiness with all beings. I did witness some of the terror of the Bangladesh Independence War (1971) and the plight of refugees, and senseless killings due to communist Naxalite movement joined by many college students in Calcutta.

In my teen years I got hooked into reading many translations of English and Russian Classics along with Bengali literature. At times, I would stare at the stars in hot summer nights lying on my back looking at the Big Dipper question mark. The mystery of the universe and our place on earth as humans was something that got me out of my limited mind to unbounded awareness. I was aware of the extensive poverty, slums, many inequalities of caste and gender and daily survival grind and indignities of the masses in much of India and developing world. The great divide between academic learning and its lack of engagement with real world suffering perplexed me. The paradox of spiritual enlightenment and material impoverishment made me feel something out of balance in our modern scientific education and thinking.

I learned much more from the five or six annual family vacations than perhaps whole year of schooling. Our first family vacation was in a Sea beach near Kolkata. My teacher told me that the Ocean is so vast; one cannot see the other shore. Seeing the Ocean elicited both awe and speechless calm within me along with a quiet wish to see the other shore. When I was around thirteen, my father's health started to decline with his asthma. He would often take our family to Bodhgaya, the place of Buddha's Enlightenment, and other nearby Buddhist places like Rajgir, Nalanda, and Sarnath. Seeing diverse tourists, monks, seekers and hippies from around the world and immersing myself in the energies of these places in the 1970s somehow shaped my inner quest for truth and happiness.

My great grand uncle Karmayogi Kripasaran (1865-1926), founder of Bengal Buddhist Association (Dharmankur) came from a very humble village background. Yet he became a pioneering figure in reviving Buddha dharma in his time in Bengal and North East India through great resolve, integrity, effort and compassion. My father aspired to preserve his legacy along with being sole provider for our family and sometimes his relatives. My parents kept their Buddhist ethical training and generosity even during times of adversity. Oddly enough by watching my dad go through repeated asthma attacks gasping for his last breath before his demise at age 58, made me keenly aware of the preciousness of human breath.

Coming to Tucson, Arizona in 1985, as a graduate student of Geography and Planning was the longest journey I ever made away from home. I got married the same year. The word 'Alien' at the LA airport immigration line stood out to me. Coming from a monsoon climate to the barren hot desert of Arizona along with pressure of new school, marriage, without contact to family, friends and mother would made me gasp, like a fish out of water. I cried my heart out for a year or more, mostly inside the closet as I learned to hide my pain well enough to show my false face of independence. I developed compassion towards immigrants and women, who go though many trials and perhaps some trauma to adjust to a different mindset, culture, food, language and environment.

After graduation I joined the Ph.D. program, yet had to leave Arizona with Maya, our 3-month-old first child and her dad with a new job in Kentucky. The very first week after we moved, it rained heavily like monsoon. I settled down focusing on raising Maya as a full time mom. From this intimate experience, I wrote a chapter titled; 'Magical Moments with Maya' in the anthology "Pearls of Wisdom: A Second Strand" compiled by Patricia Crane, Ph.D. and Rick Nichols. After two years of homebound life I started feeling restless. So I found a full-time job as a Socio-economic Planner for the Planning Division under the Mayor in my home city. First week was stressful as Maya came down with chicken pox and I felt awkward on the staff-meeting day. Being the only woman, from a different culture in a group of ten older white male planners and technicians was a lot more challenging than I thought. A drama of discrimination unfolded over a simple foolishness on the part of my manager, which I had no control over. Eventually things got painfully isolating for me that I dreaded going to office.

I could not find the cause of my inner rage and divine discontent that was building up for years and I felt my life has come to a dead end or a crossroads. For the first time since my coming to the US in 1985, I listened to the voice of my intuitive feminine wisdom, my Inner Coach. She whispered: what is your deepest desire now? I responded with three things. 1) I want to unplug from everything external and just be present fully with myself, my daughter and spouse 2) find out the cause of this inner crisis, despite having a good family, friends, a decent house, two cars, some savings and two graduate degrees. My Inner Coach said, 'just do it!' I quit my job in January 1993, in spite of having a sense that my spouse may lose his job (he did so in June). I had no way to turn but inward.

Renouncing all external goals helped me turn my senses inward, and be fully present with whatever daily rituals I did. A sense of calm contentment and peace began to fill me. This was the deliberate beginning of my seven month and seven days journey to Natural Awakening. I did not learn to practice from books or any scripture (yet it had many parallels with Buddhist mindfulness, insight meditation, stream entry and such). It was as if I was remembering something. My intention was to find out my true path, purpose and work, not the one conditioned by society, culture, parents and peers. A process of deep inquiry arose spontaneously as I stayed open with wonder and curiosity. It took me through the many layers of gross and subtle mind, form-based and formless consciousness and open empty awareness.

I could hardly do any sitting meditation with an active and playful infant. Now I am envisioning a process of mindfulness for non-monastic lay people called 'mindfulness in motion'. My favorite meditation posture was lying down, after waking up, before afternoon siesta and bedtime. I could sustain my presence most of the day connecting every hour with my whole breath-body not rushing anything, getting distracted or agitated over anything. My inner voice would guide and assure me, 'stay here' until I was ready for the next step. The last seven days my mind became so blissfully still and quiet that there was not a single distractive thought! Then there was a spontaneous Awakening, that was registered in my whole body like a second birth! It was accompanied by unearthly ecstasy of connecting to the Source, the indestructible Void, unfettered freedom of the Unconditioned, and unshakable Peace of the Deathless! My deepest gratitude to ***Buddha,*** my Inner Coach and my grandma ***Dipa Ma***, a master meditator who embodied the gentle and fearless, feminine way.

Susmita Barua, MS. MA. CPC / Dharmacharya Navasajiva, is a gifted Life Coach, Dharma Teacher, and Workshop-Retreat Facilitator of the Feminine Wisdom, Unfabricated Mindfulness and Awakened Self. She loves to teach, speak and coach single women, spirit-led entrepreneurs and planet friendly organizations to reinvent themselves, find alignment with their true purpose and mission in the world. She facilitates training on Mindful Ethical Leadership and Engaged Spirituality through practices like 'Mindfulness in Action' and 'Mindful Dialogue'. Mindfulness is a natural spiritual faculty we all have but we lose it by not using it. It is the best tool for igniting the natural genius of a person, actualizing human potential, create a peaceful world and develop synergy and capacity within a team for top quality performance and productivity. She served as Founding Board Member and President of non-profits and presented papers, retreat and workshops on various national and international forums.

Susmita Barua
www.susmitabarua.com
@linkedin
@facebook
Cell 859-420-3922

Life Coaching and The Power of Leading Questions

KNOWING WHAT QUESTIONS TO ASK

By David Cary

"Asking the right questions makes life coaching highly effective by engaging with a person at the core of their lives and leading them to a better life!" ~ David Cary

---

The value of something usually comes down to one simple question: Does it make people feel better some way? Think about it. As our resources allow, we spend our energy, time and money on things that make us feel better. If someone can convince us that some action or thing will cause us to feel good—or feel better about ourselves, we see it as something of value. This reality certainly applies to the work of life coaching. The proof in the pudding is quite simple: Coaching that is worth something is that which makes another person feel better about their life.

So the question becomes, what is the magic that makes life coaching of value? Amazingly, the power of coaching happens through a process of engagement that uses a simple communication technique known as "leading questions".

I learned about the power of leading questions the hard way.

It was a steamy August afternoon when I filed for bankruptcy in downtown Memphis. I felt whipped as I trudged into the lawyer's office. I was a single dad struggling to provide for two teenage girls. All I had was $110.00 in my bank account. The upcoming payment on our aging Chevrolet Astro van posed a big challenge, and the next month's rent seemed impossible. Though we had some well-worn furniture in our apartment, I felt penniless and was filled with self-pity and anger. Like other people struggling through life, I longed for a better way to live. There must be some guidance and solutions somewhere that would lead to a better life.

This bankruptcy was just another step down the pathway in a valley of disappointment. I had already worked through two divorces, four career changes, a failed business and two serious illnesses. The most I could feel good about was that I was a survivor.

To make matters worse, I was a "professional" who should have known better. My formal educational training was in the areas of psychology and religion. My various careers included both psychotherapy and pastoral counseling. If anyone should have known how to make the most of life, it should have been me. Instead, I excelled only as an expert on marital failure, financial failure, business failure and health failure. In short, I was a successful failure.

One question haunted me on a regular basis. How are other people moving forward in life while I keep falling behind? I was confused and frustrated. I decided to find the answer, whatever the cost!

I began to watch people who appeared to be succeeding and contented with life. I was determined to uncover their secrets and find out what I needed to do. I also went to counseling. I went to therapy. I went to church. I read numerous self-help books by best-selling authors. Finally, I found the answers I was seeking.

My help came from an unexpected source...and in an unexpected way. Simply put, my father began asking me questions. That's right. Not just kind-hearted questions of concern, but leading questions that took me down a new path. I found myself thinking about the questions he asked on a regular basis. These questions influenced my actions. The questions were truly leading questions as they led me from a bad place in life to a good place. I didn't realize it at the time, but my father had become my personal life coach.

Don't misunderstand. My father was not certified as a life coach. But he did the work of a life coach by utilizing the simple tool of, the leading question. In many ways he was ahead of his time. Though his education was in the fields of science and theology, he might as well have studied psychology. Neurolinguistic programming was clearly a part of his approach to life as he was constantly analyzing the power of beliefs, values, attitudes, actions and words. As a spiritual man, he also knew from experience the powerful influence of a God-based faith on a life. In all of his thinking, somehow, somewhere, he had realized the power of leading questions.

So, through my experience as both a struggling human, and more recently as a life coach, I, too, have learned that leading questions have the power to change life for the better. But it is not simply a matter of just asking questions. The questions must have certain qualities to be used effectively in the coaching process. What are some of these qualities?

1. Leading questions are powerful when they engage with the inner person.

The coaching process starts with a good connection between the coach and the coachee, between the helper and the helpee. Before anyone can engage in a life-changing process with someone, there needs to be an authentic relationship that provides the client with a feeling of confidence in the coach. They need to know that their coach not only cares, but they can connect by asking the right questions. If help is to come, there must be the assurance that the helper understands exactly what the person is experiencing in their lives.

Someone has reworded a quote from St. Thomas Aquinas by saying: "If you are going to help someone, you must go to where they are standing, take them by the hand and lead them."

I was always impressed that at my lowest moment, my father didn't judge or criticize or correct me. Rather, he asked the questions that engaged both my heart and mind. His questions let me know he understood what I was experiencing. He came to where I was and started working through things with me right at that point in my life.

2. Leading questions are powerful when they clarify our thoughts.

Much of our discomfort in life is the confusion we feel when working through tough times. The sense of not knowing what's going on or what to do—or what we should even hope for—creates an uncertainty and insecurity about life. If someone can help us identify what really matters or what should matter, much of the fog lifts and the sun begins to shine again in our lives.

At a certain point while working through divorce, my ex wife and I were at odds about who would assume what debt. This is obviously one of the more difficult and emotional aspects of most divorces. My father asked a question that eventually helped me sort through some of the chaos in my emotions. The question was simply, "How much is your peace of mind worth?" This question caused me to think and clarify my life values.

3. Leading questions are powerful when they provide new understanding.

So once there is a good rapport established with good credibility, and once we start seeing ourselves and our circumstances clearly, there comes a time when new understanding is important. If all we do is talk about our feelings and frustrations, we might feel some temporary relief, but we will not likely learn what is needed to move on to the better life we seek.

Early on in the breakdown of my marriage and family, I began to chase after my spouse who was running away from me—kind of like someone fleeing an accident! I was sending flowers, leaving mushy voice messages, sending cards and notes—even doing a little stalking in my desperation to work things out. I was making a real fool of myself as she had moved on and had no interest in trying to revive old feelings of love. Again, my father had some questions for me. "Dave, are you familiar with the tough love concept where if someone is being chased or pressured, they run away the faster? Do you understand that the best chances of anything good happening take place when you stop, catch your balance, get your life back under control and find the ability to live a good life on your own?"

So, as my father was asking these engaging, clarifying and enlightening questions during this difficult time, I was moving from a life of pain and weakness at Point-A to a life of healing and strength at Point-B. This is the power of an effective life coaching process—when people move on to better places in their lives.

How does someone know what questions to ask that will be helpful? This is obviously an important part of being a life coach. If the coach is not knowledgeable or experienced (an expert) in the specific area of need, they may do little more than render the comfort that comes with knowing someone cares. Of course, coaching could even prove to be harmful if someone does not know what questions to ask. It would be like the blind leading the blind. The experience of a coach is valuable as they will better know what will be helpful to another. There are also time-proven, universal "laws of life" that can be easily learned and used with leading questions—a great topic for another time and place.

To summarize, leading questions makes life coaching powerful by engaging with a person at the core of their lives—with their current values and beliefs, on their terms, in their timing, and motivated by their inner desire to act on helpful life information.

As mentioned, my professional careers included being both a psychotherapist and pastoral counselor. There is obviously a need for both professions as many people find help for life through these services. However, from my experience, there are many people who find the thought of spiritualizing or "psychologizing" their angst—to be outside their comfort zones.

Fortunately, there is another powerful option for those who seek a better life. And it involves a lot of answers!

Can you think of a time when someone has used a leading question to help you improve your quality of life?

David Cary is a certified life coach with professional experience in clinical psychotherapy and pastoral ministry. He and his wife Holley own Cary Life Coaching, LLC.

Dave has two degrees from Kansas Christian College, a B.A. in Religion and B.Th. He has written for various publications and collaborated on several books including 'Out of the Overflow' and 'Each One Teach One'. Besides speaking at seminars, businesses and churches, he has hosted a nationwide radio broadcast called 'Decision Time'.

David and Holley live in the Memphis, TN area. Together they have a blended family of two sons and four daughters.

To learn more about "life coaching and the laws of life", visit http://carylifecoaching.com.

Financial Coaching: Blending Financial Planning Analytics with the Art of Life Coaching

By Holley G. Cary, CFP®

"How a person feels about money is basic to their mindset and to the creation and satisfaction of goals and objectives." ~ Holley G. Cary

---

Working as a Certified Financial Planner™ Practitioner may not seem like the most fun career to many people. I hear all the time about how boring it would be to work constantly with math and numbers; the stock market, taxes, and all those statistics that we have to be aware of when crafting a personal Financial Plan. However, after more than 30 years in the Financial Services industry, including the last 20 years as a CFP® professional, I can tell you that this is most definitely (first and foremost) a coaching business. Preparing a holistic plan involves not just quantitative analysis, but a keen understanding of goals and objectives, and what the client is really trying to accomplish.

Having also been a Certified Life Coach since 2012, I have seen the many facets of planning and how money plays a key role in life satisfaction or lack thereof. The age old phrases, "Money does not buy happiness" and "Ignorance is bliss" usually ring true or play out in some way in my clients' lives. Finances can be anything from a centerpiece in someone's life to a topic to be avoided at all costs.

For Financial Planning to become a blend of advising and coaching, there are a few areas we have to address with or understand about our clients. We can crunch numbers and do the best quantitative analysis with the most up to date technology around, but if we don't gain understanding of these important elements, we are wasting time, dollars and possibly compromising our client's well-being.

First; we must hear from our clients their goals and objectives or what they are trying to accomplish. If we make our own assumptions, we may lead the client down a path he did not intend. We must help them to articulate what it is that is important to them and where they see their own financial future. This can be done by asking leading questions, making observations from the data you are collecting, or just being quiet and listening to their conversation. There have been many client meetings in my career where the client will bring in a well-organized data package; full of tax returns, investment statements, a completed financial questionnaire and other quantitative items. If I just took the data and used it to compile the plan, it would be like putting a recipe together; not knowing if you were baking a cake or a casserole. In these types of meetings, I usually politely compliment their preparation for our meeting, then slide the package to the side while we dive into a meaningful conversation of open-ended questions. Many times when working with a couple, the best dialogue opens up when encouraged between spouses: "Mrs. Client, what will YOU do when your husband who has travelled his entire career now retires and is now home all the time?" "Mr. Client, what would happen to your family if you become disabled at an early age? How will your wife handle the education of your children?" The responses tell me a great deal about family dynamics, beliefs about finances and how they handle unexpected events. From that, I can begin to formulate further questions which will lead us to meaningful short and long term goals and objectives.

Second, and a pivotal component to coaching a client through the Financial Planning process and beyond, is discovering the clients' "Philosophies of Money". How a person feels about money is basic to their mindset and to the creation and satisfaction of goals and objectives. One of my favorite stories illustrating what this looks like is about a very high net worth client who was working with me on his estate planning - what he wants to have happen to his fortune upon his demise. At the time, he was in his early 70's, semi-retired, and divorced with one grown daughter. His net worth was in excess of $40 million.

There are estate planning techniques utilizing charitable donations or trusts that can serve to lower federal estate taxes significantly, while providing a philanthropic outlet for substantial funds. After carefully explaining a recommended strategy for him in great detail, he leaned back in his chair and said to me, "I built the business with my own hands, sold it and now am preserving this money for my daughter. She may have more money than she will ever be able to spend in her lifetime, but I am not interested in giving anything away to anyone else; even if the tax savings is substantial." I had initially missed the mark with my client's philosophy of money. He saw the money as the fruit of his own labor and wanted to keep every dollar in the family as best he could. I had to withhold judgment on his decision, but come back to him with another strategy for his estate planning. And our relationship only got better as time went on, because I then learned to take the time to ask questions before drawing the conclusions.

Another topic of interest in financial coaching and advising is simply how a client defines "wealth". Our department within the firm I work for is called "Wealth Management". What an open concept! Those words can mean so many different things to different people. Think about it yourself for a minute…. What does it mean to have wealth? And what does it mean to "manage" it? Is it the ability to retire at an early age? Is it having a certain amount of assets in the bank or investments in your retirement plan? Is it being debt free? Or is wealth being able to buy what you want, when you want it and then give money away freely to others? For a single mom that I coached through a lengthy financial planning process, her definition of wealth meant that all three of her kids were well educated with no student loan debt, they each had meaningful employment and she was able to modestly retire by the time she was 70. The only way I knew that those were her goals, was by listening to her, getting to know her and asking her to discuss some heartfelt issues in order to create a financial plan that was meaningful to her.

The new definition to be released in 2019 of what constitutes a Financial Plan according to our governing body, the CFP Board of Standards, includes the words "collaborative", "process", "maximize a Client's potential", "meeting life goals" and "integrating personal and financial circumstances". Well, that sounds like financial life coaching to me! Until we have a good understanding of the client's heart and mind, we will miss the mark in our advice to him.

A couple of years ago, I began working with a recent widow who lost her husband after a lengthy illness. He had been a top executive for a national company with a headquarters in our city; making a lot of money. She had been a stay at home wife and mom; managing their household, raising their three sons and finally, caring for him. The husband had historically handled all the financial details in their lives and while she had been used to following his guidance, she had also been used to spending a lot of his income. Before he succumbed to his illness, he had visited with an attorney to craft a workable estate plan for her and his family. The problem became that the attorney did not offer to explain the plan to the wife and let the husband take care of that. The new plan curtailed a great deal of the cash flow and of course, the husband's income was going away due to his death. Whether it was mis-communication on the part of the husband and wife, or the simple fact that the wife did not understand the directives in the documents, we are now immersed in a two-year difficult relationship with the widow (now age 60), due to the fact that she has never understood the terms of the trust her husband left behind for her and has been somewhat unwilling to listen. She keeps saying, "That is not what he told me would happen. This is not the lifestyle to which I am accustomed." This case has become a true coaching challenge; to try to help her understand things that are new to her and to try to help her set new goals and direction for her life. Open ended questions, with an attempt to educate her has been the technique used to make progress.

A good life coach and a good CFP® professional learns to ask the hard questions. We have to get inside the clients' hearts and minds to discern what is most important to them. Since many of our clients may not understand all of the financial details and jargon within their lives, it is imperative that we learn to speak their language and show them how goal attainment can enhance their lives and the lives of their loved ones. The project is not to show how smart or experienced we are as professionals. Our unending task should be to find out "what makes them tick" and craft the best plan for their needs; revising as life events occur or the unforeseen happens. Financial Planning and Life Coaching make for a very interesting blend of careers. I have not been bored in the slightest!

What are your short and long term financial goals and some action steps that will help you attain them?

Holley G. Cary has built a successful career in the Financial Services industry and has been a Certified Financial Planning™ practitioner for the past 20 years. Working for a large regional financial institution has provided many opportunities to develop coaching skills on many levels, from managerial to working with clients on a daily basis.

Holley has a BS with a concentration in Marketing and Management from Christian Brothers University in Memphis, Tennessee. She also holds a MBA with a concentration in Finance from the University of Memphis, also in Memphis, Tennessee. Her Certified Life Coaching designation was obtained in 2012. She is active in life coaching strategies for women, including Women and Wealth, mentoring and ministry opportunities.

Holley and her husband David have a blended family, married in 2004. They share 6 adult children, 4 sons and daughters-in-law and 5 grandchildren. Together, they have founded Cary Life Coaching, LLC and work with coaching clients on many levels.

To learn more and to pick up your complementary "Spending Plan" template, please visit www.holleycarylifecoach.com.

Relationship Coaching
By Gregory Charles

"We cannot have a better relationship with others than the one we have with ourselves" ~ Gregory Charles

I finally got to a point in my life where I could own the title, Aussie Relationship Guru without pretension, but as a simple fact.

As a kid surrounded by relatives in helping professions like nurses, a priest and a monk and as a Libra I was intrigued by the ways people related and sought to learn and understand them. I saw how some people were quite effective, others very dysfunctional and needed to comprehend the differences.

This launched me on a life-long journey that has taken me around the world, into other cultures, belief systems and realities. Thirty five years ago I came upon the realization that we in fact create our realty, including the shape, tone and quality of our relationships, out of what we believe. Those beliefs arise from many places like family and social conditioning and past lives, and they in turn shape our experiences which then loop back to "prove" our beliefs. I saw that whatever we believe we will prove, and so if we do not like the outcomes, we need to own and change our beliefs!

Along the way I also came to see that we cannot have a better relationship with others than the one we have with ourselves, and so I focused in on how to grow, heal, transform and perfect our inner relationship with ourselves. This is an ongoing task for many years, no quick fixes here, as we do that more, we then can open to deeper levels of ourselves for more healing and growth. As we engage that process life, and our experience of ourselves becomes easier, clearer, safer and more beautiful - filled not with fears and anxieties, insecurities and pain, but with more and more love, joy and pleasure in ourselves and in the evolving, new relationships that naturally manifest.

Most of what we are told about relationships is either incorrect or outdated, over simplified and in denial of key components. For example we are taught to fear and avoid our fear. We are taught to fear and eradicate our physical and emotional pains, usually with legal or illegal drugs. Being a very intense person I had to find a way to actually heal and master my fear and pain. What I got to learn was that they are my Great Teachers. They pointed me to where I was wounded. They pushed me to go deeper. I realized that pain is simply intensity resisted or denied and that fear is not the issue - the problem is we learn to be afraid of our fear and so never deal with it directly.

Once we learn to stop fearing and running away from fear and pain everything changes. Instead we begin to trust our inner experience. We begin to value the lessons and messages we are given. We learn what we really need and as we provide it we also learn who we really, truly are, behind and beyond the masks we had to create to survive as we grew up.

Where to begin? Drill deeply into questions and issues like the question of: When the chips are down what is my real value? What about me can I depend on? What is my inner strength and safety net?

One of mine is simple… based on many years of harsh challenges: I never, never give up. No matter what. Period. Therefore I know, in my bones, that if things get hard I will endure and master them because… ta, da… I never give up.

Over the years I have developed many of these bedrock qualities within myself that I value beyond price… values, principles, inner disciplines, lines drawn etc. that define the quality of my Be-ing, and the quality of my being in life.

It is always a good time to focus on what you have mastered that holds you in good stead, and what other qualities you are mastering and those you value to begin mastering. A worthy path that is truly a part of real spiritual growth and development - of your Spirit, so you can live and lead a spirited life!

My baseline definition of 'spiritual' is to live life WITH spirit, in a spirited, alive, present way, with enthusiasm and excitement, and continuing to develop more and more excellent values, qualities and principles.

We are often in a deep process of inner transformation, often revisiting old emotional issues to bring them to completion in order to further our trans-form-ation. With all the changes we have gone through in life, and still are, it is important to realize we are not merely changing. We are in fact transforming!

What does that mean? Think of a caterpillar becoming a butterfly, a tadpole becoming a frog. The FORM we take in life is becoming a new expression of us as we fully show up with all of that which we have learned, developed and mastered over the past years.

Parts of you may need to wither and die to allow new qualities etc. to be born.

You are in a very real sense also becoming your truer self, a more real and authentic expression of you without self-delusion, or illusions, or false self image and thus in becoming real you may see parts of you that you do not like but now finally can deal with and change forever. That is also a huge, powerful and valuable part of your transformation. Bravo. It is the journey to become You more fully - Who you want to be and How you want to be, and that means self-acceptance, ease and flow with you in your own skin; a worthy spiritual journey. The old is dying and the new is being born.

"Before you fill the cup, first you must empty it." Zen Buddhist saying.

The down-to-Earth value of all of this is that life Be-comes easier and more enjoyable. "Problems" are easier to solve. For example a client of mine, a successful New York entrepreneur of 43 was in what he believed was a life-long loving (though challenging) relationship until the day his partner announced she needed more space and left. He was shattered. Devastated. He was referred to me and told me he thought it would take a year of weekly sessions to heal his heart, if he could. With me it took 8 weeks for him to reach deep understanding of what it was all about, including the lessons and value of it all. He got to release the pain and blame and surfaced with a new, bigger reality and awareness of himself, his needs, wants and desires and could now move on to create new, more fulfilling relationships than he had imagined possible - and had not been able to manifest until he went though his opening process.

Our relationship with ourselves goes further than that into the physical reality of our life, such as creating dis-eases. I got to see that physical dis-ease is literally pointing to emotional unease, and if we read the message we can take appropriate action, so in my healing seminars I teach people new ways to relate with their own body - i.e. another aspect of themselves, in order to create new and deep levels of ease. In the process, people have simply "disappeared" all manner of illnesses including many cancers.

The tragedy of humanity to me is that we all learned that we were powerless victims: of circumstances, of germs, of the weather, the economy and may other situational factors and as powerless victims by definition were unable to change them, so we had to go to 'experts' like doctors and priests to intercede for us. I learned that that too is just a belief and that we can learn to own that we are creators, and learn to make our own changes. From this life experience I created a mantra:

"I choose to believe

That I create every moment of my life

With love and wisdom for myself

To get value."

Just as we see dramatic changes in technologies and knowledge in the outer world, the equivalent leaps in consciousness with our inner world are now possible. Such models as psychiatry and psychology take a similar place as the Model T Ford - a marvel of their time now totally passe´. What is left is to ask yourself whether you are ready to learn these new approaches, these new techniques, to apply new beliefs and to see if you too can become a magician in your life, creating your dreams and ideals in all of your relationships. At age 66 I can now look back over my life and know I did, and that you can, as have thousands of people around the world who have learned to do so in my seminars.

It can feel scary. It can feel risky. Learning to "own" our pain and fear, to face our suppressed 'monsters' is all counter intuitive to nice, normal society which values no change, no surprises, comfort through inaction. I invite, and challenge, you to become the biggest, best, most visionary man or woman you can be, to engage in a journey of discovery and wonderment at "what a piece of work is man(kind)". You can transform your relationships with you, your family, work colleagues and the world in general if you are ready and willing to do so. That is how we become our potential. That is how we truly change the world. That is how we end inner and outer wars and strife. It is a worthy journey!

    Peace and Love! - Gregory

Gregory Charles

Over the past 35 years of world travel, study, research, exploration, and living his life to the full, he has astonished social and business leaders, academics, professionals, and others in a dozen countries with his wisdom and knowledge, simplicity, genius, clarity, humanity and availability. Gregory has met heads of State, been embraced by the Dalai Lama and had his hand kissed by a Pope.

Traveling, living and studying in many countries he has merged the best of the knowledge of the East and West - of traditional and alternate approaches - to everyday realities to have Life be all it can be.

Gregory's wisdom has helped enhance tens of thousands of lives in all arenas - love and relationships, business, family, finances, sexuality, health and wellbeing - to increase quality of life and spiritual meaning, direction and purpose.

He teaches people how to access, define and create their highest best versions of themselves and the lives that they want, over and over and over again.

This has led to him being interviewed on national TV, radio and print media, in Australia, New Zealand, America and the UK.

Gregory has also been a Visiting International Lecturer at UC Boulder, The London School of Economics and was a Consultant Faculty Member at UCLA teaching alternate healing.

You can reach Gregory at <u>WorldPlayInt@mac.com</u> http://www.aussierelationshipguru.com/

Addiction Is Just a Symptom of a Bigger Problem

"SUCCESS IN RECOVERY IS DIRECTLY CONNECTED TO LIFE PURPOSE."

By Jon Wainwright

It was a cold winter at a time long ago when the winters in Southern California were still actually cold. My punk rock band, I had put together with a friend nine years earlier, only because of his insistence that we could, had finally seen its last show. Sure we'd had plenty of hiatus's but this time it was for good.

It had been a month since the previous drummer and I had had an altercation on the 4th of July, my favorite holiday; at Hermosa Beach right on the strand no less. Tension had been mounting for some while, as he'd acquired an ego while out on the road with a bigger act than our band, and by this time I had shut our band down. He hit on my girlfriend at a bar a few weeks later, and now he had shown up with the singer of that same bigger act, to the 4th of July festivities I was playing at. Slightly intoxicated he was beckoning to play drums with the 3 piece one-off band I had put together specifically for this occasion. We were going to play ten to twelve covers and just have a good time.

Obviously I wasn't going to oust the drummer I'd been practicing with, so I told him he could sing a song if he liked. The trouble began as soon as the microphone hit his hands with his opening slogan "I'm normally in a real band."

"Wow" I thought to myself, and to think his drum kit would still be collecting dust in his parent's garage if it wasn't' for me asking him to join us.

Anyway, he sings the song and for his grand finally he spikes my microphone into the cement. Now being in my band as long as he'd been, he knew how particular I was about my equipment and he knew spiking my microphone would provoke a reaction. So as I was playing the opening licks of the next song, I gave him a light kick to the behind to get his attention and gestured "Like WTF?". That prompted him to react as I was playing that next song. He maneuvered himself behind the band and rushed in and he tackled me from behind while I'm singing and playing guitar, in front of the young mongrel gang of kids who'd become our fan base over the years. That was not very wise decision on his part. Long story short, he went home in the ambulance and I went home for the first time in a very long time with no consistent musical outlet to speak of. I was no longer the singer of the band that had become my identity and my life purpose.

So here I was, 6 months later and what had been an on again, off again, side hobby with pharmaceuticals, had grown into a Frankenstein heroin habit. Looking back on it now, I don't know what I was thinking the first time I shot up. If I was thinking, it was that I wanted to make sure the amount I had left got me nice and ripe. I had a dinner date that night. Trust me it isn't easy eating a Chinese cuisine when your face is in the bowl. What had been a one-time experimental thing had taken on a life of its own, quickly. I basically stopped caring completely. I had been supporting myself for years with a job drafting for a civil engineer and selling pharmaceuticals and hadn't worried about money in a long time.

Now my ability to function on a consistent level as a part-time drug dealer was even being threatened as I was consuming more of the product than I was distributing, ruining my income that had been a life line for me for years.

That was how this addictive craze all started. Many, many years prior, as a means to make rent and other bills whilst in school, and singing and playing in a punk rock band. The latter is where I really found my identity and respect in the music community and the only community I wanted to be a part of. I was anti-materialism, against all forms of conformity and really into stirring the emotions of the normal constituents of society. To me they were all insane and even more insane if they didn't have a vice or two to take them out of the reality that was created to enslave them.

I was never in a band to be famous or make money. I was in it to live it. But suddenly that was gone. I was a lamb without his Sheppard. Within a couple months my suppliers realized my debts were only compounding and they began to withdraw from using my distribution facilities. Up to this point my escapism was left to the weekends and parties, gigs and what have you. Now it was a fulltime endeavor, as I couldn't get far enough away from reality to feel as I once had; like a man with a purpose. Even though it wasn't a conventional purpose, it was a purpose to me all the same and carried more importance to me than any other.

"Jon the drug dealer" and "Jon the drafter" were hidden characters behind the persona. I flaunted "Jon the artist / musician" and "Jon the punk rocker". I didn't realize how much the absence of this band would affect me. I had played in many bands. Rock 'n' Roll bands, reggae bands, and other punk bands. But this band was the oldest, as it was the one my friend Bill and I started long ago as an experiment to see if we could. and the band took me on a journey I could've never foreseen. This was the one band that was a result of mainly my efforts. It gave me something to be proud of, something to be respected for, something that was attractive to women, slowly with some, quicker with others.

As soon as I stopped performing with this band something changed. The future had darkened and it wasn't as important to clean up every so often as I had been doing for over 6 years at that point. I would use the pain killers for a month or two, then kick, push through physical withdrawals that were brutal and I somehow made it through successfully. I'd done this multiple times a year, for years. However now it seemed so irrelevant of a process. I had no reason to be "on point" for. No tours upcoming. No shows. No practices, nothing. And now that I wasn't the local pharmacist any longer I graduated to using heroin. Which in reality, I didn't prefer as the high was completely different than the high energy level of pain killers I'd been using for some time. Where the Oxycontin would get me wired, prepped, pre-warmed up for any and all endeavors, heroin just left me in the second phase of Oxycontin which was the tired "nodding out" state heroin is known for.

So I was now injecting heroin and started adding cocaine to get the energetic high I was looking for, when I realized that the yearly cover-band gig I'd been doing for 7 years was coming up in couple months and practices were starting that week. The reality of the painful withdrawals I was facing hit me like a ton of bricks as the cold-turkey method I had experienced in the past were no longer an option, It was then I decided to enroll in a program. This the first time I enrolled in a state institute Methadone program. Methadone was a man-made opiate that had been produced in a laboratory during World War II as an answer to the diminishing supply of the opium poppy to make morphine for the soldiers on the battle field. It wasn't until years after the war that "they" realized the long-lasting effects of the man-made substitute would be a great answer to the overwhelming number of G.I's who'd come back from the war addicted to morphine. With methadone's long half life, the addicted soldiers could come into a clinical setting once a day and get "medicated" instead of having to "medicate" three times daily on morphine or heroin.

I had woken up at 4:15am to arrive at the methadone clinic at 4:45am to ensure I was the first in line for enrollment, as I started a new job that Monday morning at 8am for a drafting job for a structural engineer. I signed up for the smallest cycle allowed, called a 21 day detox.

All had been going well for the first two and a half weeks into the program, when the last two days fell right on the night of the gig. I ended up relapsing that night and awakening that hunger that never sleeps. It wasn't too long after that when I was driving to use at a friend's house and hit a skate boarder bombing down a hill careening into the side of my car. I fled the scene in haste worried that my car would be searched and I would be arrested. Ironically I was found and wound up in jail a week later anyway. All in all, what ended up was a new perspective on life.

I was forced to stop using and discovered a whole new world of possibilities for myself; one with a purpose anchored in spirituality and my connection to our Father and being of service to others. Focusing my life on being a good person, one dedicated to righteousness and his fellow human beings. Even in a world of self-centeredness being the order of the day, I can be that beacon that shines to the people that there is still good in the world and by doing what I know is right, whether it's helping a stranger on the street or coaching someone to find their own new purpose to pull them from the monkey that binds us to addiction. I know I leave an example that ripples out into the universe. A universe that is much smaller than most believe or realize. It isn't impossible to change this place that seems to get more and more twisted as time passes. It just takes the good people to realize there's a problem and we can only fix it together, united as brothers and sisters of this existence that can be so beautiful.

I will gladly give my life to be one of the catalysts that brings attention to the solutions to that ugliness that will only be changed through uniting all the good people of the world into one unstoppable service to aid righteousness and stop the giant evils that plague all of us. Our Father, let me and others who want to be, be the spotlight that shines on all those atrocities that conspire in darkness and let them be brought to light for all to see and choose if they're going to be a part of the solution or a part of the problem.

I see coaching as just a beginning of a world I would much rather be a part of; one that coalesces instead of competes, one that acts vigilantly and unified to those who impose their will on others, one where responsibility falls upon the shoulders of every individual instead of the state, and where people realize our Savior lives in us all, instead of waiting in vain for one to come. We were all given that responsibility when our Father gave us free will.

I live my life with a strong belief that knowing right or wrong is inherent in all human beings and it is the individual who decides to take heed or ignore them. I passionately remind everyone I meet to be kind to each other and to treat everyone as you yourself would like to be treated; it's not called the Golden Rule because it comes second or third.

My real sin would be to die without cause. I live to carry out our Father's will, not man's false interpretations of it. I will carry it out without judgment as I carry no authority over any other human, just as no human carries authority over another without the commanded giving some means of consent. "Every man is created equal" is the biggest falsehood we live in today's materialistic insanity we call society. I watch as all my brothers and sisters fight and compete to obtain the very thing that enslaves us all, money. The human race shall never be free until they take responsibility for their consent to be enslaved and realize that each individual is created in the image of our Father and no one, no one… shall be given dominion over another because to do so would disavow the one gift we are truly given in life by our Father, free will and the right to choose.

"The only thing necessary for the triumph of evil is for good men to do nothing." Edmund Burke

Jon Wainwright is a celebrated musician, painter and black ink sketch artist and deep thinking philosopher who after recovering from a debilitating opiate addiction spawned by the influx of pharmaceuticals pushed on the public after 9/11/2001 went on to find Recovery Coaching and not only help people but assisted the willing to find purposeful and meaningful lives. In 2010, he became the Master Coach for the Recovery Coach Training program at Wainwright Global after Joe Drews, one of the courses authors, handed over the reins. Jon spends his time creating art and music.

You can reach Jon at 800-711-4346 or Jon@WainwrightGlobal.com

You can enroll in Jon's Certified Recovery Coach course at www.lifecoachtrainingonline.com/our-courses/recovery-coaching/

Spiritual Coaching: A Metaphysical Approach to Self Love

By Barbara Wainwright

"Our deepest fear is not that we are inadequate. Our deepest fear is that we are powerful beyond measure. It is our light, not our darkness that most frightens us. We ask ourselves, who am I to be brilliant, gorgeous, talented, fabulous? Actually, who are you not to be? You are a child of God. Your playing small does not serve the world. There is nothing enlightened about shrinking so that other people won't feel insecure around you. We are all meant to shine, as children do. We were born to make manifest the glory of God that is within us. It's not just in some of us; it's in everyone. And as we let our own light shine, we unconsciously give other people permission to do the same. As we are liberated from our own fear, our presence automatically liberates others." ~ Marianne Williamson

---

I believe that we are all spiritual beings having a human experience. The very essence of who we are comes from our spirit, our soul, our divinity. Our spirit is the light within us that sustains us in difficult times. Our spirit calls to us to make a difference, to leave a legacy.

A successful spiritual experience opens an individual to the magnitude of all that is, which invokes an inner-awareness of our own "still small voice within" revealing our unique spiritual purpose.

Spiritual coaches help clients by being present for them and by creating an atmosphere of unconditional love and acceptance. Unconditional love allows your client to grow and expand at their own pace, encouraging them to be open to miracles that are all around us. We help our clients to discover their divine path and become aware of their own intuition, to develop trust that every experience has a purpose which leads to personal growth and ultimately enlightenment. We help our clients to identify the signs that are ever present in our lives, giving us clues to our next best step.

We respect our client's personal prose. They may call their higher power God, Angels, Buddha, Master Teacher, Jesus, Holy Trinity, Mother God, Father God, Allah, Jehovah, Yeshua, Lord, Father, Creator, Almighty, Divine Being, Holy Spirit, Maker, Yahweh, Universe, Spirit, Supreme Being, Abraham, Grand Architect, Source, or Core.

Spiritual coaches talk about things like transformation, discernment of spiritual messages, avoiding ego attachment, letting go, life purpose, universal oneness, reincarnation, our physical temple (body), past life exploration, being in the natural flow, inner-balance, being of service, meditation, self- acceptance, journaling, community, energy healing, connecting with source, living in the now, prayer, living with grace, atonement, making amends, forgiveness, forgiveness of self, conflict resolution, spiritual quests, spreading the word, contributions / tithing, stream of consciousness, law of attraction, toning, drumming, channeling, soul travel, chakras, energy work, auras, spirit guides, angels, diversity of opinion, allowing, trusting, surrender, and spiritual alignment.

We help our clients to develop their intuition where they will sense, know and understand without apparent effort. There are four different modalities of intuition: clairaudient, clairvoyant, clairsentient and claircognizant. Clairaudient intuition is when someone hears information or voices, like Joan of Arc. Clairvoyant intuition is when a person has visions, like movie scenes streaming through their mind. Clairsentient intuition is when someone senses things, a gut-feeling or touches a personal object and senses information about the person to whom the object belongs. Claircognizant intuition is when a person has an inner-knowing, they instantly understand as information is imparted to them. Typically individuals are strong in one intuitive modality, though some may be strong in all four modes of intuition. Intuition is innate. A person's intuition may be closed off or blocked, however the information is always streaming from the Universe. Recognizing intuitive signs can be learned and developed through practice.

Spiritual coaches provide tools to help our clients develop their intuition and spiritual connection to source energy. Some of the tools involve journaling, pendulums, oracle cards, intuitive exercises, flash cards, spiritual books, spiritual rituals, spiritual meditation on a question, and spiritual confirmations. These tools help strengthen your spiritual muscles and they do take practice!

Journaling is a great tool to put down in writing what is circling around in your head so you can see it and examine it. Stream of consciousness writing (also known as automatic writing) is when you put your pen on the paper and without consciously thinking about what you want to write, you write anything that comes to you.

Pendulums can be used to answer "Yes or No" questions only. You can use any object on a string, needle and thread, or a necklace for example. You ask a question as you hold the pendulum over the palm of your hand. If the answer is no the pendulum should swing back and forth and if the answer is yes it should swing in a circle.

Oracle Cards can be used to get messages directly. You ask your question and sense which card to draw. You can use the cards to gain insight, peace of mind and confidence in your decisions.

Meditation can be done many different ways, sitting, lying down, or even standing. Many of us have experienced meditation in some way or form. Meditation is most often used to clear the mind of clutter and "mind chatter" so that we feel more peaceful and aware of what is going on around us. Meditation also helps us stay in the present moment and if we are living in the present, "the now", our ego is not involved. The ego only likes to live in the past or the future where it can create a painful or fearful story for us. Meditation gives you access to your inner-guidance system, to your subconscious. Meditation is relaxing, refreshing, rejuvenating, invigorating, and can be a great aide to help you sleep. A meditation can be guided or silent. You can meditate anywhere. Some people like to meditate in nature, the bath, the shower, church, or a holy, sacred place.

Spiritual rituals are great for developing your spiritual practice. Set an appointment with yourself for the same time every day, or every week, where you show up with the intention of opening up your "clair". The appointment is a signal to your guidance system that you are present to meet with them and open to hear, see, sense or become aware of any messages they might have for you. To enhance your session, during your appointment you can light a candle, burn some incense, listen to soft music, use essential oils, and hold a quartz crystal in your hand.

A spiritual book can be a great tool to receive confirmation of a message. If you are confused about a certain issue; it is amazing how fundamental it can be to grab a spiritual book, or religious book or self-help book, and go to any page, and without looking, stick your finger on a paragraph and read it. See how it almost always will address your question and give you an answer to it. Try it. It works!

Ask for signs from your spirit guides, angels or Creator and watch and listen. You may see the signs outright. Someone may speak the answer to you without knowing it. You may read it in a book; hear it on the TV or radio. The sign may pop into your head. You may see it in a dream, or see the sign on the side of the road. The key here is, after you ask, be prepared to receive the answer using all of your senses. Look for clues.

Intuitive exercises help to strengthen our senses. For example when the phone rings, try to intuit who is calling you before you answer the phone. If you want to speak with someone, sense them calling you and note how long it takes before your phone rings. Another exercise is to think of a friend and try to sense what they are feeling, then call them for confirmation.

Flash cards are something you can create to help strengthen your intuition. You can use index cards to start with. Draw a circle on one card, a square on another, a star one another and triangle on another. Place all four cards face down before you and randomly shuffle them. See if you can discern the order of the cards. Turn them over for confirmation.

Spiritual confirmation is something you can ask your guidance for. Confirmation can come in many forms. Speak to your inner-guidance system and ask for the type or style of confirmation you would like to receive. It could be a seeing a butterfly, hearing an airplane flying over, finding a penny, lyrics from a song, a light flashing, or hearing a bell sound. For me, I've found that if I hear a suggestion three times, whether that suggestion comes from a song, a person or a book, then it is something I need to pay attention to and take action on.

There are many tools that can help you to get calm and centered so that you can connect with your inner-guidance: meditation, mantras, yoga, Qigong, Tai Chi, breath work, crystals, essential oils, sage, and placing your attention on being present in the moment.

In our Certified Spiritual Coach course you will learn the Wainwright Global Method of Coaching as well as take a deep dive into spirituality as we explore all these topics and more. If you have a passion for empowering others and you embrace spirituality, this course may be perfect for you.

Eckhart Tolle says, *"You are here to enable the divine purpose of the universe to unfold. That is how important you are!"* I also believe this to be true. I believe we are all here with a divine purpose that is unique to each one of us. Spiritual Coaching is one path to discovering yours.

As Albert Einstein said, *"There are only two ways to live your life – One as though nothing is a miracle. The other as though everything is a miracle."* It is your choice. Choose wisely.

Barbara Wainwright, the CEO and Founder of Wainwright Global Institute of Professional Coaching, is known as the most sought after teacher in the coaching and self-empowerment industry and is well-known for creating the Wainwright Method of Coaching. Barbara's life experiences have led her on a path of self-discovery and higher learning in her personal quest to make the world a better place for her family, her friends and her clients. Barbara believes that every person is born with a unique mission in life. And that once an individual discovers their specific purpose and begins taking steps towards actualizing that, a new level of confidence slowly unveils itself, many different forms of abundance become realized, and inner-peace begins its evolutionary process. Barbara is responsible for training over 6,000 professional coaches worldwide since 2006 and has established credibility in the marketplace through acquiring accreditation at the university graduate level by the Association to Advance Collegiate Schools of Business, as well as by Strategic Learning Alliance, an applied-learning credentialing organization who confers the CPC® credential of professional coaches.

You can reach Barbara at 800-711-4346 or Barbara@WainwrightGlobal.com. You can learn more about Wainwright Global's coaching courses at http://www.LifeCoachTrainingOnline.com. Download a free book about 52 Coaching Niches here: http://www.lifecoachtrainingonline.com/content/freebook.

Afterword

We trust you have enjoyed reading these coaching stories and that you have been inspired in some way to move forward in your own life. Hiring a coach may be one of the best moves you can make to ultimately have the breakthroughs to your personal success that you deserve.

If you are contemplating becoming a coach, we recommend you contact Wainwright Global Institute of Professional Coaching for your education and certification.

Wainwright Global Institute of Professional Coaching currently offers courses in Professional Life Coaching, Spiritual Coaching, Recovery Coaching, Relationship Coaching, Group Leader Coaching, NLP Coaching, Health Wellness and Healing Coaching and Career Coaching.

Wainwright Global Institute of Professional Coaching

http://www.LifeCoachTrainingOnline.com

800-711-4346

Printed in the United States
By Bookmasters